CONNECT

Pearson

The Financial Times

Pr e for Connect

'Guy and Tami's new book arrives at a time when our fundamental connectivity has rarely felt more tested nor more vital. Whatever your business challenges and goals, big or small, this book deciphers the most important ingredient of all – personal connection. RESOLVE to get your copy now!'

John Belgrove, Senior Partner, AON

'As the world in the 21st century rapidly changes around us, one thing remains constant – our work and happiness is determined by the quality of relationships that we build. This book provides an excellent, simple-to-use tool kit for helping us to connect for success.'

Dr Malte Gerhold, Chief Integrated Care Officer, Birdie Care

'In a time when true human connection is so challenged, yet so necessary, the purpose of *Connect* has never been more important or relevant. At its heart this book supports us, the readers, to understand and know ourselves better, so that we may know and understand others. It is a practical resource for businesses and leaders but, equally, a guide for all of us to rediscover and harness the power of human relationships.'

Kate Croxton, Head of Community Health Programmes, British Heart Foundation

'*Connect* deals with a simple, but often overlooked, idea – that workplaces are above all social constructs. Successful leaders don't necessarily need to have the biggest ideas or take the boldest risks, but they do need to connect meaningfully with those around them. While academically grounded, this book is easy to engage with, and full of case studies and exercises to help you strengthen your own connections and grow as a leader. I found it interesting and enjoyable from start to finish, and will continue to dip back into it. As we deal with the challenges of broken connections – socially and in the workplace – in these unprecedented times, this book could hardly be more timely or relevant.'

Richard Bowyer, Director of Marketing and Public Fundraising, Great Ormond Street Hospital Charity

'Improving our relationships is the best investment we can make in ourselves. If you want an easy-to-use development guide that details what small and consistent steps to take, this is a book you need to buy! You can read it front to back or simply choose the sections that you need most.'

Karin Wierinck, Global HR Business Partner;
Vice President, Takeda

'Building a great business is about making personal connections and *Connect* gets to the heart of the matter. Essential reading as we accelerate towards a post-Covid digital world.'

Paul Gannon, Business Development Director and
Board Member, Kainos Group plc

'Guy and Tami hit the nail on the head on today's most needed and, too often, missing skills to perform better with each other and thus as an organisation. In the digital age that bets on social networks and pure data, *Connect* reveals the underlying social skills needed to exploit one's full potential. This book is an indispensable guide for every leader which connects prevailing approaches with new practical models, that you can use right now, right here!'

Peter Weidig, Head of Holding Services,
Franz Haniel & Cie. GmbH

'What a pleasure to come across a book that starts by focusing on human relationships and affections, rather than isolated, unemotional workers, managers or clients. Tami and Guy really know their stuff, drawing on the different worlds of management and psychoanalysis with real care and rigour. They serve up their insight as an invitation to learn more about yourself and your relationships – not as the usual yell of orders and dumb certainties. Want to know more about how you and those around need to and have to connect with each other? Then crack this one open!'

John Higgins, Director Of Research,
The Right Conversation

'To connect with those around us is the very essence of effective leadership, and this book is a perfect and practical guide to how to do that fully and well. If, as a leader, you hope to inspire and enable others to give their best, then this is an invaluable read. The thinking, the tools, the exercises and the case studies give you all you need to make better connections.'

Chris Askew, CEO, Diabetes UK

'Thought-provoking read with fantastic tools and reflective exercises that brings a fresh perspective to the importance of connections and very relevant in today's workplace.'

Karen Breen, Deputy Chief Executive and Chief Operating Officer, Sussex NHS Commissioners

'Reading this at a time of global turmoil and unprecedented healthcare challenges, it enabled me to focus on the value of investing in human connections, which I have no doubt led to better decisions.'

Amy Rylance, Head of Improving Care, Prostate Cancer UK

'This book is about the art of connection – a new roadmap for human interaction for our time.'

Julian Nettel, former NHS CEO

'Why should you read this book? In a nutshell, Guy and Tami tell you what connection is, why it's essential and, more importantly, HOW to connect. An indispensable guide to a critical subject.'

Mike Brent, Professor of Practice, Ashridge Executive Education; Director of MBA Ltd

'A practical and engaging book that will help you work through the challenges we all face in working well with others. It will be particularly helpful as you move towards, or take your first steps in, a leadership role.'

David Jones, Assistant Director of Improvement Support and Innovation, Diabetes UK

'We are all connected in this world, even more so now than ever before. It's empowering to recognise our ability to choose different aspects of our personality and connection types to create the best possible outcome in a given situation, be that a one-to-one meeting, dealing with situations or even systems. Guy and Tami's book has been essential reading to improve my own connections.'

Dr Farooq Ahmad, Accountable Clinical Director,
North Merton PCN /GP federation,
National Health Service UK

'In the murky and suffocating times of global distress and division (and isolation due to conditions such as the pandemic of 2020) this book comes as a breath of fresh air. The calming and well-informed voices of the two authors provide numerous practical means to ease communication, unite the divided, and resolve impasses and conflicts that so easily fog the atmosphere of the workplace. The main theme of *Connect* describes exactly the kind of heartful manner of relating that serves to dispel the worst of the social ills that can so easily choke us. Although it is cast largely in the form of advice for the business community, the guidance offered derives from a deep understanding of core human values and, I would say, much of it is as relevant in a family home or a Buddhist monastery as it is in a boardroom. Having "good friends" (kalyanamitta) was said by the Buddha to be of primal significance in establishing well-being. This book goes a long way to describing how such true and meaningful connections, even friendships, can be made between us for the benefit of all. The words of this fine and thoughtful volume are seasonable, reasoned, well-defined and connected with the goal of well-being. I heartily recommend it.'

Ajahn Amaro, Abbot of Amarvati Buddhist Monastery

Guy Lubitsh
Tami Lubitsh-White

CONNECT

RESOLVE CONFLICT,
IMPROVE COMMUNICATION,
STRENGTHEN RELATIONSHIPS

Harlow, England • London • New York • Boston • San Francisco • Toronto • Sydney
Dubai • Singapore • Hong Kong • Tokyo • Seoul • Taipei • New Delhi
Cape Town • São Paulo • Mexico City • Madrid • Amsterdam • Munich • Paris • Milan

PEARSON EDUCATION LIMITED
KAO Two
KAO Park
Harlow CM17 9SR
United Kingdom
Tel: +44 (0)1279 623623
Web: www.pearson.com/uk

First edition published 2020 (print and electronic)
© Pearson Education Limited 2020 (print and electronic)

ISBN: 978-1-292-28687-7 (print)
      978-1-292-28688-4 (PDF)
      978-1-292-28689-1 (ePub)

British Library Cataloguing-in-Publication Data
A catalogue record for the print edition is available from the British Library

Library of Congress Cataloging-in-Publication Data
Names: Lubitsh, Guy, author. | Lubitsh-White, Tami, author.
Title: Connect : resolve conflict, improve communication, strengthen
   relationships / Guy Lubitsh, Tami Lubitsh-White.
Description: First edition. | Harlow, England ; New York : Pearson, 2020. |
   Includes bibliographical references and index.
Identifiers: LCCN 2020025295 (print) | LCCN 2020025296 (ebook) | ISBN
   9781292286877 (paperback) | ISBN 9781292286884 (pdf) | ISBN
   9781292286891 (epub)
Subjects: LCSH: Conflict management. | Organizational behavior. |
   Interorganizational relations. | Interpersonal relations. |
   Interpersonal conflict.
Classification: LCC HD42 .L83 2020 (print) | LCC HD42 (ebook) | DDC
   650.1/3—dc23
LC record available at https://lccn.loc.gov/2020025295
LC ebook record available at https://lccn.loc.gov/2020025296

10 9 8 7 6 5 4 3 2 1
24 23 22 21 20

Cover design by Two Associates

Print edition typeset in 9.5/13 Helvetica Neue LT W1G by SPi Global
Printed by Ashford Colour Press Ltd, Gosport

NOTE THAT ANY PAGE CROSS REFERENCES REFER TO THE PRINT EDITION

In memory of our loving mother

To our life partners, Iris & Flash

And

To the new generation, Ella & Ben

CONTENTS

ABOUT THE AUTHORS

This book is a collaborative project by two siblings, both doctors of psychology, with two different perspectives (counselling and organisational psychology), two different cultures (United Kingdom and Alaska, USA), two different lifestyles, coming together with one shared desire – to translate 50 years of combined workplace experience (Guy) and clinical therapeutic experience (Tami) into a practical model that helps people connect at a deep level and address the human longing for connection and belonging.

Guy Lubitsh (younger sibling) is a chartered organisational psychologist and Professor of Practice at Ashridge Executive Education/Hult International Business School, where he teaches and consults on leadership and organisational change. His work spans sectors and industries, including Novo Nordisk, BSkyB, the World Health Organization, Diabetes UK and the British National Health Service. This often involves coaching and assisting senior executives on how to improve organisational performance through increasing their ability to improve personal impact and connecting with others on individual, team and organisational levels. Guy trained in organisational consulting at the Tavistock Centre in London and is a visiting professor at the Interdisciplinary Center in Herzliya. He lives in northwest London and continuously adapts his personal communication style to connect with his two teenagers and wife. In his spare time he enjoys yoga and always seeks opportunities to sail in the Mediterranean Sea.

Tami Lubitsh-White (older sibling) was born and raised in Israel where she worked for many years as a journalist and a theatre director. After moving to Alaska, she translated the skills acquired in both professions into a new career as a psychotherapist. She completed her master's degree in counselling psychology from the California Institute of Integral Studies and her doctorate degree at Alaska Pacific University. Tami worked as a clinician with diverse populations in both in-patient and out-patient settings. She specialises in treating trauma. In recent years she moved into the new and exciting world of integrating behavioural health into primary care. She founded and managed an integrated behavioural health programme at the Anchorage Neighborhood Health Center in Alaska and is now developing an innovating approach of integrated care that connects mind, body and heart. She teaches at Alaska Pacific University, has a private practice and is certified in psychedelic assisted treatment. She looks forward to implementing this new and promising approach in helping people to heal and grow.

PROLOGUE

We just completed writing *Connect* and then a miniscule virus took over the world. This prologue is written while we are still at home adapting to a new vocabulary that is aimed at 'flattening the curve', which means reducing the number of people who are infected by the Coronavirus. Phrases such as 'physical distancing', 'social distancing' and 'self-quarantine' are now an integrated part of our vocabulary. Daily life has changed radically. Grandchildren are hugging grandparents through screens, holidays and festivals are celebrated via platforms like Zoom and Doxy and children's schools have moved to distance learning. We can participate in business meetings in our underwear as long as the camera captures only our neat shirt and tie. The 'best wishes' which used to end emails are often replaced by 'stay safe' as we anxiously witness the growing numbers of people who are infected and those who have died. Connection seems crucial, but more difficult than ever.

Leaders across all sectors and geographies are facing complex and new challenges. On the one hand, in order to survive and make profit they need to lay off millions of people. On the other hand, they realise that without humanity the situation would become intolerable. COVID-19 has created another condition, loneliness, which is spreading at a higher rate than the virus. In Zoom conversations, managers complain that working remotely is cutting them off from the informal aspect of working relationships like gossip, office politics and crucial information passed on through small talk. It is more difficult to seek advice or ask for help.

There is a sense that the future is going to be radically different from the past, but who knows! After all, we are adaptable creatures and the world might find its new normal before we will have had time to fully form a theory about it. The media is floated with possible scenarios we might be facing the 'day after'. As health care systems struggle to deal with the medical emergency, many prepare to deal with the economic, social and mental health crises that wait for us when we wake up the morning after.

There are many speculations about what tomorrow could look like, and the only thing that seems to be solid and clear is the uncertainty. Within this chaotic situation, one thing seems to shine through loud and clear, we need to connect. We need to take care of each other, and our survival as humans depends on our ability to prioritise collaboration.

Wherever this book finds you, having techniques to connect would be advantageous to deal with any situation in front of you. It will help you learn about your connector type, give you tools to resolve conflict and improve your communication with others. The last chapter addresses how to do it in the digital age.

Stay safe.

SETTING THE SCENE

We are like islands in the sea, separate on the surface but connected in the deep.

William James

The foundation of this book was laid years ago, when we, the authors, had a terrible fight. Sibling rivalry goes all the way back to Cain and Abel. We played out our own version of the biblical story. We followed the cycle of jealousy, revenge and separation that brought us to the doorstep of a known lawyer in Tel Aviv. He anticipated mediating in what seemed to be a completely lost case. Shaking his head, he kept saying 'the ultimate blessing in life is peace'. It made sense logically, but the message could not infiltrate layers of wounds, miscommunications and fears. A few minutes later, when everything seemed lost, we sat on a bench deeply engaged in a lose-lose situation. Guy, the younger, took a brave step and asked: 'Why are we doing it to each other? Why are we doing it to ourselves?' Something in his confused look, and vulnerability, started to crack years of bitter fighting. In this second, we had clarity that the only thing we really needed was to connect. We sobbed on each other's shoulders. It felt like the ending of a Hollywood film. But, by no means, was it happily ever after. Moving forward, we needed to acknowledge our complex different personalities, our shadows and confusion. We walked away from this bench with a mutual commitment to walk the sometimes complex path of connection. This event also resonated profoundly with our professional experience at work. We understood how crucial it is to guide our clients to connect with ourselves and others.

This book translates 50 years of experience into practical models that help managers, employees and people to connect deeply and address the human longing for meaningful relationships.

We argue that the most important task for people in the workplace, in times of often violent turbulence, is to share more about ourselves so we can connect and achieve those goals that matter most to us and can only be achieved in communion with others.

WHAT WILL THIS BOOK DO FOR YOU?

The following chapters will mainly address business interactions in organisations and between organisations. The guiding principles we discuss can be easily translated to our personal life and implemented in our relationships with our families and friends. Our goals are to unveil the secrets that will support you to improve your ability to connect, have satisfying relationships, and have better outcomes in your daily interactions. We suggest a set of practical techniques to make your work environment more supportive and increase your job satisfaction.

The book contains practical tools that will allow you to:

- recognise your connecting style, its strengths, challenges and implications
- gain better clarity on the quality of your connections and monitor it as it evolves over time
- connect with your whole self and achieve richer relationships – at work and in home life
- build confidence in influencing other people
- resolve conflict when tempers are running hot
- increase your repertoire of responses and flex your style to suit different situations
- work effectively in diverse teams
- say what needs to be heard when it matters
- stay curious about the world.

HOW IS THIS BOOK SET OUT?

The book is divided into several chapters. Each provides a unique perspective on connection and practical tools that allow integration of the content into your life.

The first part makes the case for the crucial role of connection. It will provide you with a way to assess the quality of your connections and recognise your connecting style, improve communication, bridge differences with others and have confidence in handling relationships.

Chapter 1 explains the importance of connection and clarifies why it is so crucial at this time.

Chapter 2 deals with the unavoidable question: if connection is so crucial to our existence, why do we all struggle with it? It describes barriers; and common traps that stand in the way of connecting.

Chapter 3 provides the opportunity to identify your personal connector style and to consider how this plays out at work and in one's personal life. Each style is a set of specific patterns that we use in handling tasks at work, making decisions, expressing ourselves and addressing conflicts.

Chapter 4 explores the dynamics with other types and gives advice on how to improve inter-style communications.

Chapter 5 describes the need to capitalise on the strengths and risks of overdone strengths. It is an opportunity for self-reflection using exercises, to avoid personal derailment and identify personal takeaways for a successful career

The second part lays out a model of connection. It will give you a practical framework and tools to understand where you are stuck and how you can improve current relationships. Chapter 6 describes the model of RESOLVE (Realise reality, Establish clear boundaries, Seek support, Own it, Listen, Validate and Evolve).

Chapter 7 outlines the principles of connection and ways to improve daily interactions.

The last part of the book looks at implementation of the tools across cultures (Chapter 8) and generations (Chapter 9). Chapter 10 focuses on how to connect in a digital age.

HOW TO MAKE THIS BOOK FRIENDLY AND EFFECTIVE FOR YOU

You can read the book from cover to cover, answer the reflection questions, complete the questionnaires, highlight tools that you want to experiment with, and make notes as you go. It can also be used as a first aid kit in case of relational emergencies at the workplace, when you have to deal with uncomfortable situations, or are in distress. You can look at the table of contents and find the chapter that corresponds with your ad-hoc need. You can start with Chapter 3 where you can complete an online connector-style self-assessment. It will provide you with insights on your unique style, its strengths as well as challenges. Further tips on how to connect more effectively with other connector styles are provided in Chapter 4. If you want to delve further into the 'shadow side' of your connector type, in Chapter 5 you can find more details and tips on how to shed light on your strengths as well as the dark side of your personality. In the second part of the book, you will find a practical framework, RESOLVE, which will help you to manage difficult situations (Chapter 6). There are further tools for improving connection in Chapter 7.

The last part of the book addresses ways to connect in various contexts/situations. Throughout the book there are activities/things you can try and do, exercises, work sheets, points of reflection and questionnaires for you to complete, if you wish. You can take *Connect* into the office, hide under the desk and pick through it as needed, you can put it on the table and invite your co-workers to join you in the mission of creating an environment that will help each one of you shine and work to the best of your talents and abilities. You can also take the book home and use it to handle domestic situations or increase your communication with friends. You can leave the book behind and carry with you the notion that we all need to be seen and respected, we all need connections. Even though it seems that disconnection is a norm in organisations, the truth is that, on a deep and fundamental level, we all seek positive connections. When what we see on the surface is conflict, discord and misunderstanding, underneath there is always a need to find a meaningful way to connect. The greatest enemies can become true friends, if we would take the time and courage to fully show up, be vulnerable and share their truth.

PART I

CONNECTION. WHAT IS IT? WHY IS IT THE KEY?

CHAPTER 1

WHAT IS CONNECTION AND HOW WILL THIS HELP YOU?

FRAGMENTED WORLD AND DIFFICULT EMOTIONS (GUY'S PERSPECTIVE)

In the process of writing this book, we encountered many moments of confusion. We kept watching the news, being triggered by the state of the planet, and having to re-commit to the concept of connect while the world seemed to be more and more torn and divided. We used current events as examples of the power of connection and the devastating outcomes of disconnect. We noticed the rise of new business models (e.g. Airbnb, Uber) which are challenging the old ways of doing things. Instead of having expensive fixed assets, business is done online by activating existing resources. Netflix allows subscribers to fully control the content that they are viewing, completely taking out the previous successful models in this sector. The promise of having a job for life is being broken with the introduction of artificial intelligence and a wider unpredictable and ambiguous working environment.

In my work, I have noticed the impact of the above on leaders. They frequently express feelings of loneliness and anxiety. Executives complain about the difficulty of staying on top of their emails, delivering targets, planning for tomorrow's strategy, satisfying clients' demands as well as handling the organisational politics.

However, most importantly, they have been preoccupied with poor relationships with colleagues, a conflict with a boss or trying to get things done without having the positional authority. Professor of Practice Stefan Wills from Ashridge Executive Management observed in the classroom that many leaders are attempting to transition into more senior leadership roles but finding it difficult to connect emotionally with their followers. Lack of connection has been at the forefront of their minds. According to a study from Totaljobs, three out of five people feel lonely at work. Of this majority, 68% say that workplace loneliness heightens stress levels and 56% say it harms their sleep. Workplace loneliness is responsible for five sick days per lonely employee per year (Mamo, 2018).

Here is a typical example.

> When facilitating a session with a top team running a major healthcare organisation, the key tension throughout the day was staff's complaint that the executives were pushing a large number of initiatives without taking into account the impact on frontline staff. They felt that issues such as work load, change fatigue, available resources and the effect on internal relationships were ignored. One of the executives had a useful insight during the workshop. He said, 'We as senior management communicate to our staff from the "head" instead of communicating with our "heart".'

THRIVING IN AN EVER-CHANGING WORLD (TAMI'S PERSPECTIVE)

One of my best friends keeps stating each time we meet that we are privileged to be living in extremely interesting times. She believes that it is a time of 'make or break' in which humanity will prevail or we will be completely destroyed. I can relate to this sense of 'living on the edge'. The discrepancy between the rapid pace of the exponential evolution of technology and the lack of significant changes in human consciousness deepens daily. We were able to put a man on the Moon and we are now aiming for Mars. In terms of our consciousness and the way we function psychologically, we have barely changed since the Stone Age. We are much better equipped to deal on the survival level, but we still love and hate, relax and stress, seek pleasure and avoid danger, connect and disconnect, live and die in the same way we always have. It creates a situation in which we are mal acquitted to deal with what the 21st century is putting on our plate.

The global priority project compiled a list of catastrophic risks. Their assessment of global catastrophic risks for 2017 included: nuclear warfare (which includes a reminder that the USA and Russia control approximately 7,000 warheads each), extreme consequences of climate change, biological and chemical warfare, catastrophic climate change, ecological collapse, pandemics like influenza (like H5N1) and the options of bio-terrorism in which people will be able to create viruses that will cause international pandemics, and AI revolution. The report suggests that we are now at a crossroads and the decisions and actions taken today will shape our collective tomorrow. As a remedy, they recommend that nations need to collaborate in order to find solutions. The Coronavirus pandemic proves the accuracy of their prediction. We believe that first people need to re-learn to connect and then nations will follow.

The external collective chaos reflects in the lives of my clients. Most Americans are suffering from moderate to high stress: 44% report that their stress levels have increased over the past five years. After years of working as a clinician, it became clearer to me that the lack of connection is the root cause of most mental health disorder. My clients taught me that behind depression and anxiety there is often a broken relationship. I have experienced this in my personal life, when a broken relationship affected everything from health, wellness and even the ability to manage my team at work. It is pretty amazing how the answer seems so simple and yet how often we miss the mark.

As we, our planet and the entire human race are facing new and enormous challenges, we need to rapidly upgrade our ability to cultivate connections. We put forward the notion that the world's biggest problems could be solved if we could truly connect. When we connect to ourselves and others, we are able to break walls and turn what was impossible to be possible. If we knew how to connect, we could improve a wide range of critical life factors like health, relationships, job satisfaction and well-being.

WHY NOW – COMMON GROUND (TAMI & GUY)

The noticeable differences between people also highlight the similarities. Guy has found out that the need to connect is the number one issue managers and leaders are grappling with. His clients would often say 'at the end of the day, it's all about relationships'. Initially, it was surprising to him. While he offered leaders and managers different tools, they kept discussing their challenges connecting to their organisations, co-workers and followers. Slowly, something new started to form. He understood that as humans our sense of connection is the driver behind our level of engagement, which tidily corresponds with business performance.

When Guy provided his clients with practical tools to connect to themselves and others, he noticed how other business issues that were seemingly unrelated, complex and unresolvable became manageable.

A healthcare organisation was asked to reduce its budget by 10%. Initially, top executives protected their own turf. By building trust and connection, they came together. They were willing to compromise and work creatively to find a solution that minimised the impact on the whole and allowed the revision of the budget. During the negotiations, connections created the goodwill needed to bridge different commercial business models and conflicting needs. A CFO of a building company explained that he prioritises building relationships with his business partner, banks and clients. He said, 'It is hearts that seal the deal.'

Research by the Center for Creative Leadership (CCL) in North Carolina revealed that the main reason why executive careers derailed is related to a poor ability to form relationships rather than cognitive skills and abilities (Gentry, 2016). The number one reason that psychologists burn out is the failure to connect to clients in a way that fosters change coupled with difficulties feeling connected to their agency (Raquepaw & Miller, 1989). While Guy was trying to figure out how to help leaders of organisations connect, Tami was looking for ways to improve the clinical outcomes of her patients. She was puzzled by the fact that some of her patients with considerably minor disorders did worse in psychotherapy than other patients dealing with much more complex diagnosis and prognosis. This was similar to Guy, who had found some managers able to cope with seemingly impossible situations, while others seemed to fall over in the slightest breeze. In many cases, the difference lay in the individual quality of connection with others.

While teaching her students different treatment methods, she kept telling them that, 'it is all about the relationship'. It is clear to both of us that we all need connection and it is crucial for individuals and communities, in both personal and professional life. Furthermore, we wanted to put forward the notion that the world's biggest problems could be solved if we could know how to connect. This is a big statement that we can't prove. But what if it is true?

Figuring out the how to connect is a tall order but it is possible.

CONNECTION IS . . .

When you type *connect* into Google, it yields around 10 billion results. It is higher than health and in line with love. There is a wealth of definitions but no universally accepted definition of what connection means. Based on our practice and observation, connection is an experience that has an emotional quality that indicates the presence of a relationship. A positive connection is a feel-good experience, which encourages us to collaborate, continue to relate, get closer, approach and go the extra mile. A negative connection experience can evoke difficult emotions and make us want to attack, protect and distance ourselves.

The scientist Matthew Lieberman (2015) claims in his book *Social* that our need to connect is as fundamental as our need for food and water. Not only humans but also mammals are profoundly shaped by social environment. A threat to social connection registers in our system as a survival threat. It activates our sympathetic nervous system as much as facing a wild animal. Pat Shipman (2010) suggests that animal connection is the underlying link among the other key behaviours and that it substantially influenced the evolution of humans. Connection was and still is a key to survival. In terms of evolution, Homo sapiens, who could not connect, could not survive or pass on their genes. We needed to connect in order to reproduce and we needed to be part of the tribe in order to stay alive, have food, shelter and experience basic safety. Being rejected and expelled from the tribe meant death. We also needed to distinguish between a friend and a foe. Research suggests that the feeling of connection is developed early on in humans to let us know that we are safe (Rock, 2008). Hogan (2007) argues that we are mostly ourselves in human interaction.

The concept of attachment and connection was a main focus of researchers throughout modern history. In 1943, Maslow argued that safety and belonging are at the top of the hierarchy of human requirements next to physiological needs. Bowlby, in the late 1960s, emphasised the critical role of attachment of mother–child for the healthy growth of individuals and their capacity to develop effective relationships (Bowlby, 1969). Later on, Ainsworth (1973) defined four basic forms of attachment (i.e. secure, insecure avoidant, insecure ambivalent resistance, disorganised). In the workplace and in life, we encounter people that seem as if they do not need connection. However, it is clear that it is a form of protection and, in essence, we all have a fundamental need to connect. This need manifests in different ways. John Cacioppo, a neuroscientist, pioneered a new academic domain that bridges between Biology and Psychology. He argued that love and social connection are what matter. Cacioppo dedicated his career to understanding loneliness, belonging and connection. He claimed that our neural and genetic makeup supports interdependence over independence (Brown, 2018). He said in an interview with *The Atlantic* magazine in 2017, 'Being with others does not mean that you are going to feel connected.' He explained millionaires and billionaires, as well as top athletes, tend to feel lonely. Many people seek their friendship but they still feel isolated because they cannot trust others' motives, which may be driven by social and/or materialistic benefits.

Managers invest large amounts of time and effort on clarifying mission and vision, communicating the messages to employees and, yet, more often than not, they struggle to genuinely create the experience of connection with their employees. They overlook the emotions layer which leads to a profound sense of missing the mark. It is also the reason that the top search on the Virtual Ashridge resource is on topics dealing with collaboration. For many years, it was a common belief that in order to be successful, you needed to run organisations as machines with rules and regulations and wrap the package with a thick layer of rationality. It was a good idea if you ignored the complexity of the task, the ever-changing context and, most importantly, the irrational aspects that govern human behaviour. It is becoming clearer that the main fuel that makes things work is emotion.

The reason many managers are slow in integrating this insight is that they don't know what to do with it. The requirement to connect emotionally requires them to connect internally, which is scary to many, mostly because of lack of knowledge of how to do it and the fear of what they will find inside. The key to creating effective working environments, job satisfaction and productivity is dependent on our ability to connect emotionally with ourselves and others.

SUMMARY AND ACTIONS

- Our neural and genetic make-up favours *connection* over *isolation*.
- There is a trend of disconnection at the workplace. In order to reverse it, we need to take risks and exchange real emotions of friendship.
- Communicating from the 'heart' rather than the 'head' is key to success.

Action plan:

- Reconnect to yourself and others.
- Read the rest of the book.

CHAPTER 2

WHAT ARE THE COMMON OBSTACLES AND FEARS?

Of all the liars in the world, sometimes the worst are our own fears.

Rudyard Kipling

A s human beings, we have a fundamental need to connect. In the workplace, we can benefit from creating deeper meaningful relationships in whatever role we have: managers, leaders and followers. It seems a simple, no-brainer route but the reality is that most of us are experiencing major threats to our ability to connect. If it is such an important factor, why do we stumble in creating and maintaining it in our personal life, workplace, politics and internationally? The reward of positive connection affects everything from engagement and productivity to health, well-being, longevity and yet most of us struggle with it.

There is a simple explanation, the one that explains why we don't engage in many behaviours that can potentially improve our quality of life and well-being, like diet, exercise, rest. We have a natural tendency to take the easiest path, the one that would feel good in the short term. Yet, being connected feels good, so why don't we prioritise it?

This chapter will give you the ability to:

- understand the risks of negative connection
- become aware of key external and internal barriers for connection. Some of them will be applicable to you, some won't, and some might be food for thought and catalysts for future actions. Becoming aware of our barriers and obstacles naturally renders itself to improving connections.

First, we want to look at an example of the consequence of having poor connections in a well-known case.

WHAT HAPPENS TO ORGANISATIONS WITHOUT GOOD CONNECTIONS?

When Fred Goodwin, in the mid-2000s, initiated a merger between the Royal Bank of Scotland (RBS) and ABN AMRO, he neglected to take into consideration the need to connect and consult with his own senior management team. Under his leadership, the organisational culture became one of greed and fear. Top executives reported they were encouraged to forge signatures of key customers. The atmosphere in the bank was toxic, which meant that senior leaders were frightened to challenge the CEO. In response to any dissent, Fred Goodwin reacted aggressively and made them redundant. This resulted in the worst merger in corporate history, with lawsuits and a loss of billions. Fred Goodwin was stripped of his knighthood and will go down in history with the unflattering label of 'Fred the Shred' (Robinson, 2012).

Linder, Cross and Parker (2006) studied how social networks drive change and innovation. They conducted a social network analysis on RBS in the mid-2000s which showed that several individuals were highly connected (for example, 47, 12 in the following figure) and therefore had a great deal of influence and information. However, there was a senior leader who was totally disconnected from others. Guess who?

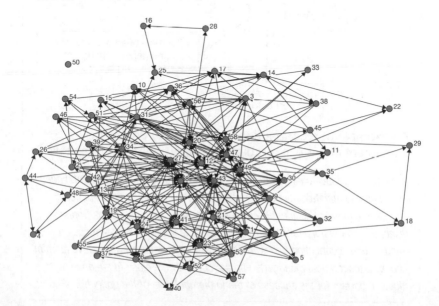

EXERCISE

It's your turn to create your own connection network. You can use it to see how your relationships are impacting you, and which connections you might need to improve to achieve your goals.

1. *First, on a blank page, make a circle that represents you and write your goal. For example, getting a promotion, improving team productivity, executing a change plan or focusing on well-being.*

2. *Then, place all the people you interact with at work around this circle. Place people, key stakeholders, organisations that are important to you closer.*

3. *Later, draw a line between you and others. If it is a good/supportive relationship, draw a straight line and if it is a conflicted relationship, draw a dotted line (see a sample diagram below). Please be aware that what you consider 'important' or 'less important' stakeholders can change over time. This map can help you navigate the landscape and prioritise your actions.*

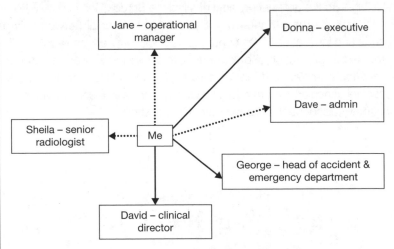

An example of a connection network – my goal is to implement change in a radiology department in a hospital

In order to introduce change effectively within the radiology department, I need to continue to maintain my positive relationship with David (clinical director) and George (head of accident & emergency department), as well as Donna (executive on the hospital's board). However, it is imperative that I focus on improving my connection first with Sheila (senior radiologist), then Dave (admin) and Jane (operational manager), who are currently not close to me and are highly important for the success of the implementation of the project.

Try today to do your own connection network

■ Identify the relationships that are currently significant and your existing connection with them and vice versa.

Now that you can see it:

■ How does it feel?

■ Is there anything you would want to change?

Throughout the chapters, we will refer to this map and suggest ways on how you can use it. We recommend doing this exercise after reading the book.

Remember: lack of connection has far wider consequences than just financial.

WHY CONNECTION IMPACTS THE BOTTOM LINE

Engagement at work is the holy grail of every business. However, a recent Gallup report revealed that 13% of workers are actively disengaged and have miserable experiences at work. This is the lowest percentage since 2000. Engaged employees are innovative and always have an idea or two about what they can do better. Unengaged employees often have an idea or two on how to sabotage organisational performance (Harter, 2018).

Gallup's measure of engagement uses 12 key questions. Their questions focus on having the tools/equipment to do the work, recognition of performance and personal development. Half of the other questions in their questionnaire directly relate to connection.

EXERCISE

See below some of Gallup's questions. Can you try to answer some of these questions on how you feel at your current workplace? After answering the questions below, can you think about how this impacts on the organisation's bottom line?

- *Do I have a best friend at work?*
- *Does my supervisor, or someone at work, seem to care about me as a person?*
- *Does the mission of my company make me feel my job is important?*
- *In the last six months, has someone talked with me about my progress?*

The above questions relate directly to the connectivity of employees to others at the workplace as well as to the wider organisational mission and values. Our goal throughout the book is to explain what we can do in order to dare to care, create an environment where people support each other, and develop closer relationships at work.

The lack of connection is especially visible when dealing with the role of line managers. They are squeezed in the middle (Oshry, 1999) and have a critical role in connecting between the mission, senior management and frontline staff. Branding and culture expert Denise Lee Yohn (2017) explains that middle managers, 'wield the most influence on employees' daily experiences'. When properly equipped, engaged and empowered, middle managers enhance overall performance: productivity, customer and employee retention, and team alignment to the company mission and strategic goals. When they are disconnected, the entire organisation performs poorly, resulting in loss of productivity, lower morale, increased attrition or all of the above. Zenger and Folkman (2014), in an influential *Harvard Business Review* article, reached a similar conclusion. They researched 320,000 employees across different sectors and found out that the most disengaged population in an organisation was 'the people who were stuck in the middle of everything'. However, organisations across the board do not invest in this critical layer of the organisation. Munch (2017), chief clinical director, Institute for Healthcare Improvement in Boston, USA, claims that even in a complex healthcare environment, senior management is reluctant to invest in middle management development, which results in poor execution of strategic plans and a waste of resources. Management in both Google and Netflix understood this.

Google, known for its informal working environment, allows engineers and developers to take 20% of their time to spend on innovative projects. The underlying message for the engineers is that Google trusts middle management connection to the wider organisational strategy and therefore will know how to use their time effectively. Indeed, it is a known fact that half of their new product launches can be traced back to 'innovation time'. It can also explain why Google is at the top of *Fortune* magazine's list of best companies to work for multiple times.

Netflix tasked line managers to play an active role in shaping the organisational culture. McCord (2014), HR director of Netflix, explains in a *Harvard Business Review* article that 97% of their employees are connected to the overall strategic vision of the business and will do the right thing. As a result, there is no formal system of taking time off at Netflix. Instead, employees can take time off when they feel it's appropriate. Bosses and employees are asked to work it out together, with an overall guiding principle that is to act in 'Netflix's best interests'. This trust has yielded a significant improvement in both employees' productivity and willingness to go the extra mile. There is a new generation (i.e. millennials) coming to power that is adamant about bringing new values to the table. They want to feel connected to organisations with social values/mission as well as demand opportunities for growth and development (Honoré & Paine Schofield, 2012). Ignoring their core values will have implications on the quality of the organisational talent pipeline and consumer loyalty.

EXERCISE

Questions for reflection

From a scale of 1 (low) – 10 (high), how do you perceive the level of engagement of staff in your organisation?

1	2	3	4	5	6	7	8	9	10

From a scale of 1 (low) – 10 (high), do line managers in your organisation view themselves as the 'guardians of culture'?

1	2	3	4	5	6	7	8	9	10

Are you paying enough attention to how you recruit and retain the new generation/millennials coming into work? Mark your answer on a scale of 1 (low) – 10 (high).

1	2	3	4	5	6	7	8	9	10

From a scale of 1 (low) – 10 (high), how supported do you feel at work?

1	2	3	4	5	6	7	8	9	10

If you scored:

40: excellent (your organisation is well connected)

35–40: good (there are some good practices but you can do better)

below 35: need improvement (see recommendations on how to improve organisational culture and connections in Part III).

LONELINESS CONTRIBUTES TO POOR WELL-BEING AND PERFORMANCE

Dan Schawbel (2018), *The New York Times* bestselling author, argues that we live in the age of isolation. EU figures suggest that, in the UK as a whole, 13% of the population lives alone. Denmark has the highest proportion of single-dwellers, at 24%. In Germany, Finland and Sweden, that number is just below 20%. Recent research by the British Red Cross showed that there are nine million lonely people in the UK. They are struggling to make social connections and experience feelings of isolation. They are worried that no one will notice if something bad happens to them (Barr, 2018). Dr Andrew McCulloch, chief executive of the Mental Health Foundation (cited in Barford, 2013), argues that, 'It's not because they are bad or uncaring families, but it's to do with geographical distance, marriage breakdown, multiple caring responsibilities and longer working hours. We have data that suggests people's social networks have got smaller and families are not providing the same level of social context they may have done 50 years ago.' This has led Theresa May (former UK Prime Minister) to nominate for the first time in history a cabinet minister for loneliness to address this phenomenon.

The wider societal problem around loneliness has been permeating into today's workplace. A recent study by CNN News (Vasel, 2018) revealed the significant impact of loneliness on the productivity of organisations. Lonely employees have a lower job performance, are less committed to the company and seem less approachable to their co-workers. Within the study, Professor Hakan Ozcelik (2018), from the College of Business Administration at Sacramento State summarises this phenomenon. First, there are fewer human interactions at work, which lead to feelings of isolation and loneliness. Second, if you are not close to anyone, even working in the middle of an open-plan office can feel lonely. Within the same study, Professor Barsade from Wharton School (University of Pennsylvania) adds that, if we do not pay enough attention to feelings of loneliness, other people will mimic these behaviours. Loneliness can spread like a virus across the organisation. To reverse this downward trend, it is important to exchange real emotions, which are critical to friendship.

We will elaborate on this in Chapter 6 where we discuss the RESOLVE model as a tool to create meaningful connections.

Guy experienced the above first-hand when working with an organisation that has over 60% of staff working as home workers. During the leadership development programme, employees reported that they value the flexibility offered by working from home and at the same time revealed feelings of isolation and loneliness, which were impacting productivity, morale and well-being. The human resource function decided to proactively address this problem and delivered well-being and health sessions with plenty of opportunities to discuss coping strategies. They alerted line managers to this organisational problem and provided a budget for staff to travel and reconnect face to face with each other.

We have found that the problem of loneliness is much more complex for high-performing senior leaders (mostly men). They find it hard to admit their weaknesses, feelings of loneliness and to seek help. Instead of discussing their emotions, they become more isolated in the workplace. There is a shift in the City of London with more understanding of the importance of emotional resilience and the popularity of mindfulness/relaxation courses (Norton, 2015). This is a positive change but still seems like a plaster on what is a much bigger problem.

EXERCISE

Questions for reflection

- *Do you have systems and procedures to detect burnout and loneliness?*
- *Do your middle and senior managers discuss well-being/burnout/health as part of the usual business?*
- *Do you take care of yourself?*
- *Do you role model self-care to others?*

If you want further information in this area, please read the self-care for leaders section in Chapter 5.

EXERCISE

Try to experiment each day this week with connecting with someone new to you within your existing social network at work. Try to find out something you did not know about them and their work.

Post-experiment reflection questions:

- *What was the experience like?*
- *What was challenging?*
- *What was beneficial?*
- *What did you learn about yourself and others?*

FOCUS ON THE TANGIBLES PREVENTS POSITIVE CONNECTIONS

Reynolds and Lewis (2017) argued that the quality of interactions is important to both the formulation and execution of strategy. In the business world, they claimed, there is not enough consideration of some of the more 'intangible' aspects of quality of interactions across the organisation. Instead, we tend to focus on the organisational structure/charts, new initiatives, teams and lose sight of the importance of some of the processes 'beneath the surface'. They coined this pattern as the 'Tyranny of the Tangible'. Emotions such as anger, fear, envy, as well as happiness and sense of achievement are shoved into the corners. The same fate awaits beliefs and doubts about yourself. They all get locked in the 'intangible/irrational box' and are put aside as irrelevant. However, the reality is that emotions and core beliefs govern our behaviour as much as the tangibles, such as cash flow and productivity measures.

When facing significant strategic dilemmas, senior managers prefer to reorganise the organisation, choosing to focus on what is under their control instead of dealing with the ambiguity of emotions. This is exactly like the joke about the person looking under the light for a penny he lost somewhere else. He is reluctant to search in the dark, even though that's where the penny dropped.

Ruth is an employee in the financial sector with 15 years of good service and is loyal and respected. She asks her line manager for a few extra holiday days to complete coursework for her Masters course:

- Response A – favour granted. Ruth feels great, relieved and her mindset is encouraged by a positive signal. It reflects on her feeling of connection to the company and desire to continue to contribute and go the extra mile.

- Response B – Ruth's request is treated respectfully and in a timely manner. Her manager explains that there are some difficulties granting her leave at this specific time but that they will work with her to find alternatives that will support her and meet her personal needs, while taking into consideration the overall company's constraints. The manager acknowledges that she might be disappointed and validates her feelings and, in doing so, opens the door to negotiation on possible solutions.

- Response C – favour declined. Ruth feels frustrated and disappointed by what she perceives as another negative chip away at her mindset. It reflects negatively on her feelings for the company and desire to lead and get involved with work.

More often than not, organisations fail to understand the importance of the intangible factors such as morale, being heard, validation and sense of commitment. These requests are usually dealt with by an accountant mind who does not know how to record the value of engaged employee to the business.

John Belgrove, senior partner, Aon Hewitt

The search for control and measurement has been one of the key reasons for the 'target culture' in the English National Health Service. Patients' needs and quality of service were ignored at the expense of delivering short-term targets (West, 2018). A study by The King's Fund revealed that this culture created a dominant 'pacesetter' leadership style among senior leaders, which is focused on achieving targets without consideration to group dynamics/interaction and trust between team members. Pacesetter leaders set high-performance standards, but neglect the relationships within the team. They roll up their sleeves and lead from the front rather than delegating to others (Fillingham & Weir, 2014).

EXERCISE

Questions for reflection

- *Do you feel safe to express your emotions at work?*
- *How do you react when others express feelings at work, such as anger, sadness or joy?*
- *Does the organisational culture pay attention to 'intangible' aspects of the organisation, such as morale, emotional safety, motivation, emotional connection with mission and values? Do you have specific examples?*

DYSFUNCTIONAL CULTURE

Culture is the water we swim in, the environment that surrounds us and dictates what is right, what is wrong, and how we live life. Schein (2017) describes culture as comprised of different levels. On the visible level, you have artefacts such as buildings, furnishings, dress codes and mission statements. Though, more importantly, 'under the surface' we have norms and behaviours that act as the glue that connects our families, organisations and communities. These are patterns that evolve through our everyday interactions, beliefs and meanings. They are learned, shared and reinforced through conversations, language, bodies, symbols, politics, rituals, stories, customs and technologies among other things. Is it OK to be late? Who gets to talk? Is conflict open or subtle/nuanced? Who makes decisions? Is this language/term OK to use or not? (Wiggins & Hunter, 2016). Over time, these can be taken for granted and become difficult to contest. When challenged, the people who lead the intervention are perceived as 'difficult', 'weird', 'awkward' and sometimes 'irrational' because they are threatening the status quo and the inherent fabric/need for connection.

Management thinkers such as Amy Edmondson (2012) argue that in order to effectively challenge established cultural norms, it is important to create a climate of psychological safety in which people can express themselves without fear of sanction.

> Guy, who has been working with the English healthcare regulator, the Care Quality Commission, has found overwhelming evidence for the link between leadership and the ability to authentically connect with staff and performance. 94% of healthcare providers who have been rated by CQC as good or outstanding overall are positively correlated with good or outstanding leadership and a culture which focuses on connecting with staff (CQC website).

Correlation is not causation and yet the lived experience of being connected and trusting supervisors and leaders showed a consistent impact on safety, patient satisfaction, medical outcomes and overall productivity.

Irving Janis (1982) coined the term 'groupthink'. It is an example of how people ignore crucial information because of the pressure to join a collective defence mechanism of denial and avoid conflict over different points of view. Janis showed how experienced leaders can lead a group of people to overlook crucial information and he mentioned the Bay of Pigs invasion, the Cuban Missile Crisis and the attack on Pearl Harbor as examples to groupthink.

When the Challenger space accident happened over 30 years ago, we were reminded of the power of groupthink. Although the engineers at NASA were aware that the shuttle would explode, they were not able to convey the message to senior management. After putting a man on the Moon, senior management was caught in arrogance and groupthink, which prevented critical information from being taken on board, resulting in a grave accident. Schwartz and Wald (2003) argue that organisations have not learned and groupthink is still alive.

Kodak, despite having the technological knowledge of the digital camera, was too slow to react on this information and go to market. The company lost out to the competition and it took many years to turn the business around. Commentators relate this lack of adaptability to a culture that required people to conform to the views of senior management (Anthony, 2016).

Recently, Guy has been working with a top team that decided to become more courageous and challenge some of the unhelpful organisational patterns that were impacting behaviours. They decided that, when there is a difference of opinion, they will learn to disagree well rather than brush their differences under the carpet. The new CEO encourages staff at all levels to use 'dutiful audacity', take risks and challenge the status quo (the phrase 'dutiful audacity', to take risks and challenge the status quo, was mentioned by/taken from the CEO of the Care Quality Commission, Ian Trenholm).

Syed (2016), in his influential book *Black Box Thinking*, provides the example of the Mid Staffordshire NHS Trust to highlight the difficulty of healthcare as a sector to learn from mistakes and improve performance for the benefit of patients and staff. The inquiry into the failure of Mid Staffordshire revealed a culture/leadership of non-disclosure and defensiveness of failure at all costs, resulting in catastrophic consequences to patients' safety, unlike the airline industry, which turned around the rate of accidents. In 2014, out of 36 million commercial flights only 210 people died (Syed, 2016).

In the healthcare sector, there are many examples of the lack of systematic and independent approaches to dealing with mistakes/accidents. The traditional power differentials between the professional groups (e.g. doctors, nurses and other healthcare professionals) limit the ability to speak truth to power and challenge authority (Atul Gawande in Syed, 2016).

The defensive culture in the healthcare sector manifests itself in lack of learning opportunities and systematic difficulties in trying out new ideas and learning from failure. Staff members are worried about being blamed for improving and challenging existing practices.

EXERCISE

Try this today:

- *Are there signs/organisational patterns of disconnection/arrogance within your organisation, especially within the senior management team?*
- *Are poor behaviours by senior leaders 'tolerated' by staff? Do staff feel safe and able to 'speak up'?*

> *Next week, try this:*
>
> ■ *Choose an area in your organisational culture that you are concerned about, and have an informal conversation about this topic with a colleague whom you trust. What did you learn?*

INTERNAL BARRIERS TO EFFECTIVE CONNECTIONS

TRAUMA AND ADVERSE CHILDHOOD EXPERIENCE

When we open the door to the office, we bring with our talents, knowledge and experience, also our hopes, fears, past and present failure and success, our history and our childhood experiences. For most of us, childhood is a mixed bag of good and bad experiences. Some experiences cast a long shadow on our ability to perform at work, feel safe and connect. People in the workplace don't wear their childhood wounds on their sleeve and yet those experiences highly affect everything they do from 9–5 (or any other window of time that we spend at work).

Adverse childhood experience (ACE) is one of the most important studies related to the effect of childhood trauma and neglect. The study led by Dr Vincent Felitti and Dr Robert Anda was conducted from1995 to 1997. 17,000 Kaiser Permanente (health insurance company) patients were surveyed before their physical exam with a primary care medical provider. The survey contained 10 questions about patients' childhood experiences, including having experiences of physical, sexual and verbal abuse, physical and emotional neglect, having a family member diagnosed with mental illness, addicted to alcohol or other substance, or incarcerated. It asked about losing a parent to separation, divorce or death. The survey also inquired about the history of sexual, physical, emotional abuse and neglect. Each positive answer got one point, so patients' ACE score was from 1 to 10.

The findings showed that patients who experienced four or more adverse childhood events had significant increased risk for smoking, increased risk for depression and suicide/attempts, poor self-rated health, greater likelihood of sexually transmitted disease, and increased challenges in physical inactivity and obesity. The study also found a correlation between a high ACE score and health conditions like increased risk for broken bones, heart disease, lung disease, liver disease, and several types of cancer.

In an article published in *The Permanente Journal* (2004), a group of researchers examined the relationship between a high ACE score and three indicators of impaired worker performance (serious job problems, financial problems and absenteeism). They surveyed 9,633 employees. The results indicated a strong correlation between ACE score and worker performance. They stated in their conclusion: 'The long-term effects of adverse childhood experiences on the workforce impose major human and economic costs that are preventable. These costs merit attention from the business community in conjunction with specialists in occupational medicine and public health.' They also suggest that dealing with workers' adverse childhood experiences would address the root origin of these problems in the workforce.

In the workplace, our small and big traumas are triggered daily. They are present in the way we interact with our peers, managers and the people we manage. We are wounded beings going to work.

Guy worked with Patrick, a CEO who experienced childhood trauma. Patrick's father passed away unexpectedly when he was seven. He had to grow up quickly and support his mother and younger siblings. This trauma shaped his leadership style. He tended to rescue his peers (senior managers) when they struggled with their role, he had difficulties delegating and was functioning in the shadow of feelings that something bad is going to happen. Eventually, something did happen and the company needed to downsize. Patrick was unable to function as he was not able to fire people. When he became aware of his wound and its effect on his decision making and behaviours, he was able to do his job. He made hard decisions, saved the company and fired people respectfully.

It is important to remember that the fact that you are reading this book right now indicates the presence of resilience, which is the factor that helps us deal with adverse experiences in the past, present and future.

PROBLEMS IN SENSORY PERCEPTION AND COGNITION

Research by neuroscientists suggests that our perception of other people is instinctive. We confirm our mental models by using our voice, body language and face. Most of the time our perception is incorrect. It drives people to emphasise data that confirm their beliefs and to discard information that conflicts with their worldview. Executives emphasise evidence that their plans work and defend against any contrary data. If you're an optimist, you'll verify your positive viewpoint at every opportunity; if you're a pessimist, you'll find many reasons to see most situations negatively. Steve Peters describes this instinctive phenomenon as 'the inner chimp': the animal inside us decides on action before we formulate a more emotionally intelligent reaction (Peters, 2012). Mehrabian showed that when there is inconsistency between the words used and tone of voice and facial expression, we privilege and trust the message conveyed by the tone of voice and facial expression instead of the actual contents of the message (Mehrabian, 1981).

Neuroscientists explain that these errors in perception are due to our social needs, which are treated in the brain in a similar way to the need for food and water (Rock, 2008). Our brain networks and behaviours are organised by either minimising threat or maximising reward (Gordon, 2000). When a person encounters a stimulus, their brain will either tag the stimulus as 'good' and engage or their brain will tag the stimulus as 'bad' and avoid/disengage. The approach–avoid response is a survival mechanism designed to help people stay alive by quickly understanding what is good and bad in the environment. The amygdala, a small almond-shaped object that is part of the limbic system, plays a central role in this process. The amygdala will be activated proportionally to the strength of the emotional response (Phelps, 2006). When a boss appears threatening, or perhaps does not smile, suddenly a whole meeting can feel dangerous and people will not want to speak up or take risks.

In a meeting, the principle of approach–avoid will be triggered by what our brain work perceives as friends or foe. Somebody feeling threatened by a boss who is undermining their credibility is less likely to solve complex problems and more likely to make mistakes. The reduced cognitive ability is related to the sense of threat and loss of overall executive functions in the prefrontal cortex and less oxygen and glucose available for brain functions which impacts memory and problem solving (Arnsten, 1998). Just speaking about somebody higher in status is likely to activate an approach–avoid response.

Conversely, Fredrickson (2001) argues that when people experience positive emotions, they perceive more options when trying to solve problems that require insight and collaborate better. Relatedness involves deciding whether others are 'in' or 'out' of a social group. People like to form 'tribes' where they experience a sense of belonging. Information from people perceived as 'like us' is processed using similar circuits for thinking one's own thoughts. When someone is perceived as a foe, different circuits are used (Mitchell et al., 2006).

This explains why our judgement of other people is made on guess work and assumptions rather than hard evidence. Research into job interviews reveals that we make decisions/judgements about people as soon as they walk through the door. Despite all of this evidence, we are often very confident of our ability to judge other people – whether on their competence, honesty or whether we like them or not (Cook, 1998).

When we treat someone as a competitor, the capacity to empathise drops significantly (Singer et al., 2006). A handshake, swapping names and discussing something in common, be it just the weather, may increase a feeling of closeness by causing the release of oxytocin (Zak et al., 2005). Relatedness is close to trust. The more people trust each other, the stronger the collaboration.

EXERCISE

Try this today:

- *Think of someone within your immediate network that you 'dislike'. Can you try and use some of the above suggestions to increase connection and trust? (For example, share something personal about yourself, offer support, ask them questions about their interests and/or recent success.)*
- *What did you learn?*

WHAT TO DO NEXT

You may find it useful to dip into Chapters 3 and 4 that help you identify personal connector types and how to communicate across people with other connector styles. Chapter 6 has the RESOLVE model that can help you handle a difficult relationship. Chapter 7 has seven ways to create positive connection. Both Chapters 8 and 9 offer tips on how to improve connections across generational gaps and cultures. Chapter 10 has useful tools on how to stay connected in a digital age.

SUMMARY AND ACTIONS

- Positive connection is fundamental to human beings and closely correlated with individual health and well-being. We continuously seek connection and, at the same time, have difficulties relating to and getting along with others.
- There are internal and external barriers for positive connection.

■ Companies that invest in creating positive cultures for staff have significantly better staff morale/well-being and bottom-line performance. Conversely, destructive organisational culture can result in poor communication, low productivity, lack of innovation and, in some cases, can contribute to tragic outcomes.

■ It's important to become aware of the tricks that your mind can play and personal biases that may impact negatively on your judgement and decision making.

Action plan for improving connection:

■ Identify whether the barrier for connection is internal or external. If it's internal; does it remind you of past negative experiences?

■ You can also examine your connector type (Chapter 3) and improve your self-esteem and ability to connect with others and/or employ the RESOLVE model in Chapter 6 that helps you handle a difficult relationship.

■ If it is an external barrier for connection, ask yourself, is there something I can do about it? Look at Chapter 8 connecting across cultures and 9 connecting across ages. In addition, you will find useful tips in Chapter 7 on the seven ways of connecting and Chapter 10 (connecting in a digital age).

CHAPTER 3

WHAT TYPE OF CONNECTOR ARE YOU?

The more a personality theory can be for a person rather than about a person, the better it will serve that person.

Dr Elias Porter

This chapter will help you identify your connector type. Once you know who you are, you automatically connect to your areas of strength and other areas where you need support. It should help you understand why, in certain situations, you are doing great, while in other situations, all your efforts seem to be falling short. One of the most important (and yet neglected) aspects of an organisational culture is the ability to recognise and embrace people's differences. It requires creating a safe environment where managers (and the people they manage) can become aware of themselves, have a voice and be able to recognise others for who they are. Such an environment empowers people to utilise their strengths, and seek support when needed. In organisations, or departments, that master the ability to create this kind of culture, employees' morale is high, productivity soars and bottom-line results are maximised. Those organisations are healthier and contribute to everybody's well-being. It sounds simple and yet naïve and unrealistic. One of the reasons for the hardship we experience in the workplace is the fact that we are often blind to the aspects that motivate us, to our needs, and what we can contribute. Knowing oneself is a first step towards the ability to function better in the workplace. It is the cornerstone in resolving conflicts and creating a productive work environment. It is really about understanding personality first.

This chapter will give you the ability to:

■ understand what we mean by connector type

- *identify your connector type and understand how it can help you*
- *become aware of the four connector types and recognise typical behaviours.*

SHORT HISTORY OF PERSONALITY

When putting together IKEA furniture, some people will first read the instructions and follow them step by step. Others will systematically ignore the instructions and follow their intuition and will read the instructions when everything else fails. The difference is called personality, the unique set of qualities that make us who we are.

The word personality comes from the Latin word *persona*, which originally meant a theatrical mask. Hoffman (2002, p. 8) defines personality as 'the unique and enduring bundle of motivations and needs, attitudes, and behaviour tendencies that makes each of us who we are'. The attempt to solve the mystery of what make us is documented in ancient history. Hippocrates (460–370 BC) believed that human moods, emotions and behaviours are caused by body fluid: blood, yellow bile, black bile and phlegm. Later, Galen, a Greek physician and philosopher, developed this concept and attached temperaments to each of the four fluids.

- Sanguine (blood) temperament is lively, optimistic and carefree. This temperament lends itself to behaviours like risk taking, love of adventures and the tendency to break the routine.

- Phlegmatic (phlegm) temperament seeks interpersonal harmony and close relationships. Phlegmatic people tend to avoid conflict and take on the role of mediators.

- Choleric (yellow bile) temperament tends to be goal-oriented, practical and straight-forward.

- Melancholic (black bile) temperament lends itself to being extremely orderly, accurate and having a tendency to follow tradition.

At the end of the 19th century, the physiologist Wilhelm Wundt explained that the four temperaments are four dimensions of human personality.

Modern psychology gladly picked up the baton of personality research and ran with it in a different direction. Carl Jung (1921), a swiss psychologist, was the first to pioneer the idea that there are normal differences between how people function. The natural preference for one of these functions over the others leads individuals to direct energy towards it and to develop habits of behaviour and personality patterns. The resulting predictable patterns of behaviours – in dynamic with the other mental functions – form psychological types. During the period after World War II, Briggs and Myers, mother and daughter, built on Jung's concepts and developed the Myers–Briggs Type Indicator™ (MBTI) with the objective of promoting human understanding and avoiding loss of human potential. Hogan (2007) builds on this work and argues that one's personality type is the bedrock of each person's psychological being and the way by which each person guides and interprets his/her life.

UNDERSTANDING THE ROOT OF PERSONALITY

Most theories of personality development speculate that personality forms an interplay between temperament and environment. The set of interpretations, reactions, habits and behaviours that together constitute our connector type developed early on as a way to protect ourselves. As children, we were all overwhelmed in one way or another and needed to find ways to cope. While one child learns to distract, another child learns to deal with anxiety by being goal-oriented and self-reliant. After practising fending for oneself, this child will become a director. A child that gets scared when parents are fighting would learn to be a mediator in order to restore peace and harmony. When things get too much for another child, they go inside themselves and learn to keep their thoughts to themselves. They learn to collect details and plan and be ready for whatever happens, and a specialist is formed.

This perspective is important because it helps us to understand why we are so identified with our connector types. Those approaches worked in our past and we practised them for many years. They assist us in understanding our own behaviour as well as becoming empathic to others. This helps us to connect to others in a deeper and more meaningful way. Furthermore, this aids us to re-evaluate our own behaviour, cultivate compassion and find more adaptive ways to cope. The ability to be aware of oneself is the path to freedom and choice. When we become aware of our connector type and its impact on others, we can start modifying our behaviour to get the result we are looking for. This kind of understanding opens the door to connect and respond in a manner that is much more productive and impactful to achieve collaboration and mutually agreed goals.

THE FOUR CONNECTOR TYPES

The four connector types are:

1. Director (gets things done).
2. Facilitator (creates harmony).
3. Innovator (makes things better).
4. Specialist (makes the right decision for quality).

We have developed the connector types, being inspired by many personality theories and perspectives and our experiences with our clients. We wanted to give you a quick and practical way to connect to your own connector type as well as understand others. It is always optional and advisable to seek more information and increase self-awareness. This connector type tool is quick, easy and practical. It can help you gain rapid insights into any situation and, by doing so, improve outcomes.

To help you identify your type, together with the psychometric unit at Ashridge Management Education, we developed an online questionnaire. The items were developed based on each connector behaviour used to handle tasks at work, make decisions, express ourselves and resolve conflict.

The tool was then distributed to managers working in various sectors who were attending courses across Ashridge's Executive Education programmes. The questionnaire was then validated, based on over 300 responses using an exploratory factor analysis. The reliability of the four connectors was assessed by analysing Cronbach's alpha of the items.

You can identify your personal connector type by visiting https://public. virtual.ashridge.hult.edu/section/connector_type. A hard copy of the connector questionnaire is provided in the Appendix.

Connector type	Score
Director	
Facilitator	
Innovator	
Specialist	

EXERCISE

What is your highest score/connector type (see explanation of each connector type below). Can you please write down two to three key reflections on the implications for work and creating meaningful relationships with others.

1.

2.

3.

It's important to be aware that, as individuals, we can relate to all types of connectors and our personality is not one-dimensional. We all have all the connector types; it is a question of how dominant each type is in our tapestry. When we talk about a specific connector type, we mean that if this type is dominant for you, you would be able to relate to most qualities. In most cases, we can't be dominant in all types and therefore need diverse teams with a combination of all connectors. This is especially important when we are delivering complex tasks. For example, an innovator type will need a director type to make sure that his/her ideas are translated into a final product. See Chapter 4 for more information on how different connectors connect.

Furthermore, each connector has a particular bias/lens through which they interpret the world. For example, a director type may view the facilitator type on occasion as both weak and over-emotional. Vice versa, the facilitator type will, most probably, view the director as, at times, too harsh and lacking empathy.

People are complex entities and we need to be aware that a 'label' of connector can't fully describe another human being and their nuances. It's important that we do not over-simplify complex human interaction. There are many other important influences/variables that need to be considered, such as culture and age. We'll provide further information on these important topics in Chapters 8 and 9.

DIRECTOR CONNECTOR TYPE

- **Basic motive:** to achieve the goal. The director type is motivated by the need to 'get things done'.
- **Main strategy:** control.
- **Characteristics:** they like to organise projects, operations, procedures and people. They are determined and like to act and get things done. They live by a set of clear standards and beliefs, make a systematic effort to follow these, and expect the same of others. They value competence and efficiency. They enjoy interacting and working with others as long as they are responsible for meeting deadlines and completing assigned tasks. People with a dominant director type feel comfortable with planned change, structure and predictability.
- **Strength:** they usually have a strong presence. They are reliable in terms of getting things done. They usually are competent and knowable on how to find the information that they need. Most of them look confident regardless of how they feel.

- **Challenges:** they may struggle to deal with emergent and unexpected change. They have little patience with confusion, inefficiency and halfway measures. Many of them find it difficult to express emotions and be vulnerable. They operate under a lot of 'should'.

- **Triggers:** they are confused when others are expressing emotions and/or when they perceive others are taking too long to react. They are triggered by silences and situations in which they perceive they have no control. They are triggered when things are not done the way in which they believe things should be done.

- **In meetings:** they are focused on outcomes and high energy. They prefer a structured agenda with each agenda item being discussed and with follow-up actions with specific timelines and action items for each team member. They are extremely annoyed with small talk which they deem a waste of time and resources.

- **Decision-making process:** their decision making is both fast and expedient and may view the consensus-building process as a waste of time. They like to depend on data but don't want to have too much of it. They usually evaluate ideas based on an objective criterion which heavily relies on how practical these are in practice.

- **Change:** they are willing to change if they understand the purpose and the destination.

- **Famous people:** Jack Welch, Margaret Thatcher and José Mourinho.

Sam, dominant type: director

Sam is a product manager within an international organisation. In meetings, Sam would tend to hurry up conversations because of her need for closure and outcomes. She is described by her line manager as aloof and cold when interacting with others. Her main difficulty is that when making decisions, she does not consult enough with others. During the coaching process, Guy has worked with her to try out different approaches. Sam experimented with allowing time for people to connect informally before the meeting, and discuss some of the emotional issues that they are experiencing at work. Agendas for meetings were co-designed together with team members, allowing space for informal conversations and making human connection. Sam has become more aware of her need to drive meetings/results, she has learned to appreciate different styles/inputs in her teams. When dealing with more complex issues, she is now more relaxed and open to listen to other perspectives.

FACILITATOR CONNECTOR TYPE

- **Basic motive:** to create harmony.
- **Main strategy:** being attuned and attentive to other people's needs.
- **Characteristics:** they are highly empathetic and attuned to others, compassionate and use their EQ (emotional intelligence) to quickly understand emotional needs, motivations and concerns. They can be inspiring leaders as well as good team members who maintain harmony. They are interested in relationships and have a good understanding of how groups and individuals work. They are natural mediators. They are adaptable and like variety and new challenges. They are exceptionally insightful into possibilities. When change is introduced, their main concern is how it will impact relationships. When communicating, they tend to listen to and support others but also have definite values and opinions of their own. They bring enthusiasm and intensity to creating strong relationships. Others view facilitators as sociable and with a large circle of friends. They value authentic and intimate relationships and, at times, will take on other people's emotions and work, which may result in burn-out and stress.
- **Strength:** they are good listeners, attentive and loyal to the people they are close to. They value people over outcomes and create a positive working environment. They are sociable and value others.
- **Challenges:** they are sensitive and at times vulnerable. They can lose sight of the goal and they have difficulty saying no.
- **Triggers:** being sensitive, they have thin skin and have the tendency to get hurt easily.
- **In meetings:** they are warm and friendly. They want to make sure that everyone has the opportunity to express themselves. They are motivated by being liked and are in need for approval from others. They take responsibility for organising interactions with colleagues, friends or family so that everyone is involved. They prefer a collaborative and engaged decision-making process and prize harmony and cooperation. Feelings guide their decision making rather than rationale thinking and data. They are happy to support other people's ideas, in particular, when they can see social benefits for the team/organisation or the wider world.
- **Decision-making process:** they are slower in making decisions as they tend to avoid conflict. They prefer to listen to different opinions before making decisions. They need to have a quiet space in order to be able to hear their own voice.

- **Change:** they accept the change as long as it brings safety and harmony to people around them. Usually, they are not resistant to change but need time to adjust. A gentle and soft environment during transitions is helpful for them.
- **Famous people:** Mahatma Gandhi, Nelson Mandela and Mother Teresa.

Rebecca, dominant type: facilitator

Rebecca is a natural facilitator. She is both warm and friendly. She is very much liked by others and values authentic and intimate relationships. Nevertheless, she tends to take up other people's problems/work. When interacting with others, she is pleasing others at the expense of fulfilling her own needs. She ends up with too much work, is frustrated with her colleagues and has recently started to miss key milestones. During the coaching work, Rebecca has learned to set boundaries on her work and, in particular, pay attention to her tendency to please others. She is in the process of learning how to say no to others' requests and take care of herself. She has decided to take up some physical activity three times a week and spend more time with family.

INNOVATOR CONNECTOR TYPE

- **Basic motive:** to make things better, to improve and change.
- **Main strategy:** they love complex challenges and readily synthesise complicated, theoretical and abstract matters. They have global thinking and dreams for the future. They are focused on visionary ideas and concepts. They are independent problem solvers. Innovators are comfortable during change, ambiguity and exploration.
- **Characteristics:** they usually have high energy and are often restless. Many of them appear as daydreamers but, once they have created their general structure, they devise strategies to achieve their ambitious goals. Their plans can be complex and not always very practical. They are capable of mobilising resources to make these ideas happen. Innovators thrive on change/ambiguity and are comfortable with emergent plans.
- **Strength:** contributing with innovative ideas. They are the dreamer, the people that are many times ahead of their time. They have a unique way of thinking and their passion is often contentious. They are quick thinkers.

- **Challenges:** they have difficulties with practicalities. Most of them are allergic to forms and bureaucracy. They have the tendency to break the rules and, as a result, they get in trouble in organisations. They are often distracted and find following through a challenge.

- **Triggers:** routine. Little and/or no opportunity to contribute to projects and an emphasis on keeping to deadlines.

- **In meetings:** they express creative ideas, innovate, generate excitement and 'outside of the box' thinking. Innovators are restless and willing to challenge the status quo. Their presentation is ever changing, they can appear logical and rational and, a minute later, they can embark on a vision that seems completely out of touch. They struggle with a structured agenda and will tend to jump from one topic on the agenda to another.

- **Decision-making process:** when making decisions, their focus is on big ideas. They do not like a long decision-making process or discussions on minor/mundane issues. They prefer integrated decision making, drawing on various aspects/areas. They will get bored by following through on actions. They may find it difficult to follow up on issues/actions and do not like details and mundane tasks.

- **Change:** they actively seek change even though they may often feel tired by their own pace of new ideas.

- **Famous people:** Steve Jobs, Leonardo da Vinci and Richard Branson.

Shirley, dominant type: innovator

Shirley is an innovator type and leads a small R&D team whose main task is new product development. When coaching her, it has emerged that the team complains about the manner in which she runs meetings. Given her strong innovator type, Shirley prefers to brainstorm rather than go through a structured agenda. Her team has become frustrated by the lack of follow through on key actions and lack of closure. Shirley seems happy to explore ideas without committing to any actions. In the coaching process with Guy, she learned to flex her connector style and pay much more attention to the planning of meetings and closure on key actions so that she can deliver projects on time, keep her team motivated and avoid losing credibility.

SPECIALIST CONNECTOR TYPE

- **Basic motive:** to make the right decision for quality.
- **Main strategy:** move slowly, collect data and avoid making mistakes.
- **Characteristics:** they are practical, sensible and realistic. They have a strong sense of responsibility and great loyalty to their organisations. Specialists are dependable and interested in applying their knowledge and expertise. They will do what is necessary to perform their job correctly and achieve a high-quality outcome. Most of them tend to be introverted. Specialists prefer to work alone and be accountable for the results within an environment where both jobs and roles are clearly defined. Creativity is not an area of strength, but they will be happy to support others with innovative ideas/projects, provided enough data/ facts rationale is provided.
- **Strength:** they are good at contributing knowledge and facts. They are systematic, reliable and knowledgeable.
- **Challenges:** they tend instead to overthink. Many of them experience communication problems. They have difficulty making their voice heard.
- **Triggers:** when they are required to process a lot of information quickly, and when they don't have time to process and collect what they perceive to be enough data to make a decision. They fear making mistakes and are worried when working outside their area of expertise.
- **In meetings:** they talk when asked. They take time to reflect before talking. They will use logic, relevant content and data in their arguments. They will come across as careful as they thoroughly apply a logical criterion based on their experience and knowledge. They are more comfortable providing input on their area of expertise rather than on general strategic areas. They do not like 'small talk'. They are perceived as consistent and orderly and run meetings accordingly.
- **Decision-making process:** when making decisions, they will want decisions to be grounded in both data and expertise.
- **Change:** they accept change if they can continue to contribute employing their expert knowledge. They prefer predictable change, which allows them to bring their expertise into play. They are not interested in change for change's sake. They will support change only when facts demonstrate that such change will bring better results.
- **Famous people:** Isambard Kingdom Brunel and Hippocrates.

Craig, dominant type: specialist

Craig is a senior accountant who is working within an international organisation in the construction sector. He is unassuming, introverted and an expert in his subject matter. Craig is now seeking to move into a more senior role which requires much more people management. He has a specialist connector style and 'people management' is not his strength. Through the coaching process, Craig learns to view that navigating the complexity of organisational politics and networking is part of his skill set and responsibility as a senior manager. He is now experimenting with meeting other senior leaders for informal catch ups, focusing on how to form a peer group of allies across the organisation and learning how to connect different people across departments to support organisational innovation and delivery.

Recognising styles

	Director	Facilitator	Innovator	Specialist
Appearance	Self-disciplined, dressed well and formal, less interested in informal conversations, straightforward	Smiley, sociable, trying to please, persuasive and enthusiastic	Has a lot of energy, is in a hurry, informal dress, jumps from one thing to another, looks different	Quiet, introverted, unassuming, honest, clear boundaries between work and private life
Voice	Straightforward and direct tone, likes pace and can be cut and dry, fills in the silence	Pauses to express feelings, gentle, warm tone	Enthusiastic, animated, fast paced, less comfortable with silence	Calm and measured tone, pauses to think, silence is natural
Manner	Formal, straightforward, dominant, focused and serious	Casual, friendly, approachable, laid-back, unthreatening, warm, smiley, may be seen as intrusive	Impatient, dreaming reflective, rushes through things	Quiet, slow pace, thorough and considerate

▶

	Director	Facilitator	Innovator	Specialist
Core belief	It's important to get things done, it's worth the risk to go ahead and decide	It's worth engaging others and getting buy-in for the way forward	It's worth sharing ideas	For the best quality outcome, it's worth integrating all the data and information
Priority	Formulate a plan and get things done	Engage others to achieve results	Brainstorm, energise	Gather information and data
Potential talents	Organising and leading, monitoring	Facilitating and hearing about people's emotions/ values/desires	Creative ideas to complex problems	Defining and clarifying
Wants to	Keep the task on track	Facilitate the group and ensure commitment	Renew the group with new ideas	Support the group process with data and expertise
Gets stressed by	Long introductions, slow pace and silences	Open conflict, lack of appreciation of their contribution	Details, rigid plans and/or little opportunity to contribute, lack of perceived 'big picture' thinking from others	Informal conversations, contributing to broader issues that are outside their areas of expertise, work that is not backed up by data/ evidence

SUMMARY AND ACTIONS

- We all have connector types that define our motivation, needs and how we interact with others.
- In order to create positive connections, you need to be aware of your connector type, which helps you to continue to build on personal strengths and increase self-esteem.

- To improve relationships, you need to continuously improve your self-awareness of your connector type and recognise others so that you can achieve mutually agreed goals.

- It's vital to own your connector type while being sensitive to other connector types.

Action plan for improving connections:

- Think of something that you want to achieve in your next meeting (e.g. increased budget, support for a new business case, introducing new IT system). Who is the key person? Using the table above, can you identify their connector type?

- How can your connector style help you (e.g. get things done, ensure harmony in the room)?

- What may be challenging for you (e.g. director: keeping silence; specialist: conversations on general topics)?

- What are the connector types of the other key people in the meeting? What may be the implications on how you would start the meeting (e.g. choice of words, body language)?

CHAPTER 4

HOW DO DIFFERENT CONNECTORS CONNECT?

Talent wins games, but teamwork and intelligence win championships.

Michael Jordan

CONNECTING IS KEY TO BOTH INDIVIDUAL AND TEAM SUCCESS

Cohen and Bradford (2005) in their book Influence Without Authority argued that in order to achieve mutual goals people continuously exchange 'currencies'. The most valued are: inspiration, task, position, relationship and personal. They explained that knowing what matters to you and others can help you achieve better outcomes in a much more participative style. If a key stakeholder in a project has an inspiration currency, it would be useful for you to use language and examples of how the work will impact wider society. Similarly, understanding yours and others' connector type can contribute to improved team communication and performance. For example, a goal-oriented manager can disclose to others his/her preference for getting things done as well as any personal difficulty with slow pace, reflection and silence. This can help others understand the manager's behaviours and flex communication (e.g. be more on point). In return, the manager can learn, over time, to value reflection and slower pace as a valuable aspect of effective group process for achieving bottom-line results. Tami and Guy, being aware of their different connector types, still needed to jump through the hoops in order to work together effectively.

Guy (dominant director type) was preoccupied with the deadlines for the publisher while Tami (dominant innovator type) was continuously adding *new ideas and content. As you are reading these lines right now, they eventually succeeded in doing it but not without overcoming challenges: openly discussing differences and finding the willingness to collaborate across personal differences.*

This chapter will give you:

■ *the tools you need to achieve mutually agreed goals while satisfying yours and others' main incentives, drive and motivation, depending on your personal connector type.*

■ *the ability to increase your self-awareness as it will make you naturally more mindful of inner motives, preferences and the connection between body language and personality traits.*

■ *the ability to boost your confidence when creating alliances in environments where you do not have the positional power.*

■ *the ability to enhance your ability to put together healthy teams while celebrating and building on natural areas of strength.*

■ *an improved appreciation for diversity, which will increase your personal ability to react due to a new-founded internal flexibility.*

Things to take into consideration before we embark on the journey of understanding others:

■ Our connector type is only one facet of our personality.

■ We have a dominant connector style and we also have traits of other connector types, which is the reason we can truly understand someone else's dominant type.

■ Avoid jumping to conclusions. In order to understand someone else, we need to suspend judgement of what is 'good' or 'bad' and, by doing that, we increase our ability to really 'see'.

■ We can improve our awareness of identifying connector styles and develop meaningful relationships through practice.

HOW TO CREATE A HEALTHY TEAM

A healthy team consists of people with different dominant connector types. Robertson (2005) argues that people's personalities differ in terms of how they contribute to the growth cycle of organisations. Every process has a natural arc. It has a beginning, middle and end. The beginning starts with an idea, an abstract thought, then there is a production phase which turns the idea into fruition. Each production requires a dreamer who would initiate the idea, then a producer who would create a plan and execute it. Within the process there is a need for a mediator who would connect between stakeholders, and a scientist who would provide data and verify that everything is going according to the plan. As people we have all those capacities, but each one of us is more connected to a specific aspect of the process. A well rounded and effective team needs people who own all those skills. Below is further information on the unique contribution of each connector type, which can help you put together a high-performing team.

CONNECTOR TYPES!

UNITE!

IDENTIFYING CONNECTOR TYPES IS THE FIRST STEP

She had a way of seeing the beauty in others, even, and perhaps more especially, when that person couldn't see it in themselves.

J.K. Rowling

Hopefully, by now, you already know your connector type (see the table below for details and there is further information on the four connector types in Chapter 3). You can identify your personal connector type by visiting https://public.virtual.ashridge.hult.edu/section/connector_type. A hard copy of the connector questionnaire is provided in the Appendix.

Four connector types

Connector type	Incentive, drive and motivation
Director	Helps you become more effective in achieving goals
Facilitator	Assists you in connecting to others
Innovator	Engages others with your ideas
Specialist	Helps you gain confidence and finds ways to get the data you need in order to improve quality

The next step would be to increase your awareness of other people's connector type, identify a potential break in communication, and find ways to collaborate in a way that would enhance people's strengths. The ability to understand someone else, to see the world through their eyes, to validate their positive, can help resolve unnecessary conflicts and opens the door to outstanding results. The sense of being misunderstood is a big contributor to feeling lonely, disconnected and unmotivated. In order to thrive at work, we need to feel safe, be recognised, have a voice, contribute and be validated. We need to have the tools to cope when things are going wrong because they will.

Ready to embark on this journey? Let's go!

FIVE WAYS WE SABOTAGE OUR CONNECTION TO OTHERS

Understanding others is a powerful tool and also a tall order. One of the barriers in forming teams and managing others is neglecting to acknowledge personal differences. When we become aware of differences, we often lack the tools to know what to do in order to make things work. We start with exploring barriers because our awareness of the challenges can help remove them. When we are trying to understand other people's behaviours, we are subject to five different biases and challenges:

1. **We assume we are alike.** We have a tendency to overestimate the degree to which others are similar to us in the way they think and behave. This phenomenon has a technical term, namely false consensus effect. We consciously and unconsciously assume that others think like we do, need what we need and feel like we do. When we lack information about another person, we tend to project our inner world onto someone else. We assume that internally they are like us while, more often than not, they aren't.

2. **We attribute our mistakes to situational factors and others' behaviour to their personality.** A classic example is when I am late, I tend to attribute it to situational factors like, it was raining, the bus was late, and there was a traffic jam. When someone else is late, we tend to believe that it is part of their personality.

3. **Fear blinds us.** When we are afraid, we will have difficulty assessing situations and people accurately. Fear is a big obstacle in our ability to understand others. There is a physiological reasoning to the fact we cannot reason when we feel fear. There is a decreased activity in our frontal lobe, the thinking part of the brain, in order to allow us to fight or flight. When we are in a flight and fight mode, it is challenging to be able to relate, understand, or analyse someone else.

4. **We get stuck.** When we are attached to an outcome and/or to a particular point of view, we are less likely to be able to be accurate in our assessment of others, also we are more likely to miss important information. There are 1,000 roads that lead to Rome; being aware of only one road would limit our ability to get to Rome. Furthermore, there are 1,000 ways to find what we were looking for in Rome in other places.

5. **Our judgements are based on limited information.** This is
   objectively true. We form a theory about what is happening. Our
   judgements are based on limited information. Please remember to just
   hold on to this lightly.

If you want to explore some of the other internal and external barriers to
connection, further information is provided in Chapter 2.

EXERCISE

*Doing this exercise can lead to significant insights. There should be a time
where just addressing our subjective truths could clear the way to better
connection and resolution of conflict. Many scientists and comedians have
commented on the fact that we are our worst enemy. Increasing our awareness
of what we bring to the table would instantly clear our vision.*

Identify challenges

*What is the main challenge I am facing right now? Rate yourself based on the
following questions where 1 is low and 10 is high.*

How motivated am I to solve or change this situation?

1	2	3	4	5	6	7	8	9	10

Am I willing to devote time to connect with the other stakeholder?

1	2	3	4	5	6	7	8	9	10

*Do I feel fear? If yes, rate it from 1–10, where 1 is low to non-existent and 10 is
high.*

1	2	3	4	5	6	7	8	9	10

*What is my main fear (e.g. fear of getting fired, excluded, demoted, ridiculed,
shamed, ignored and/or loss of status/power and/or not achieving my goals)?*

_____

How attached am I to a specific outcome?

1	2	3	4	5	6	7	8	9	10

Are there any actions I would like to pursue?

1.

2.

3.

IDENTIFY THE DOMINANT CONNECTOR STYLE IN OTHERS

We assume that, by now, you know your own connector style. The next step is to identify other stakeholders' connector types. We have reviewed the benefit of doing this. Practically, there are two ways to do it: one is to answer the questionnaire as if you are this person, the other is to use the following table as a shortcut.

	Director	Facilitator	Innovator	Specialist
Approach to informal events (e.g. drinks, dinners and away days)	Waste of time unless they lead to productive work-related outcomes	To get to know more personal things about my colleagues	Excellent platform, to share ideas and initiatives	Prefer not to attend, unless they are focused on my areas of knowledge and expertise
Appears	Strong and determined	Warm and wanting to please	Approachable	Cold and distant
Tone of voice	Direct	Enthusiastic	Expressive and imaginative	Gentle and patient
Body language	More rigid	Soft	Flexible	Distant
Speed of speech	Quick	Slower to moderate	Moderate	Slower
Gestures	Direct	Expressive	Can be both contained and expressive	Contained
Conflict	Prefer conflict to be resolved quickly, in order to complete the task	Avoid conflicts, in order to maintain harmony	Happy with conflicts that facilitate new ideas	Prefer conflicts that are based on facts (instead of emotions) and support quality

Try this today:

- Choose three key stakeholders on a current project (both 'supportive' as well as 'challenging').
- Classify yours and their connector type using the information provided in Chapter 2 together with the observation table above.
- What are you learning?

BUILDING RAPPORT WITH DIFFERENT STYLES OF CONNECTORS

In every relationship, the first few steps are fateful for creating an effective and trusting working alliance. We often arrive at these interactions with positive intentions but, unfortunately, people judge us not by our intentions but by our actions. It is extremely valuable to pay attention to our intention as well as feelings. Furthermore, there are many variables that we can't control, including the other person's gestures and reactions, though we can be responsible for our preparations and actions. Boaz and Fox (2014) argued in an article, 'Change leader, change thyself', that any organisational transformation starts with the senior executives' willingness to change themselves, challenge individual and collective mindsets and role model the new required behaviours in line with the new strategy. They encourage leaders to look inward and examine inner motivations, habits of thoughts, emotions and behaviours in certain circumstances and their impact on others. Finding the common internal tendencies that drive behaviour is a good start.

To help with this, we would like to offer a brief overall orientation for each connector and several tips on how to build rapport as well as words/sentences that you can use to ensure deeper connections.

What directors want:

- To get things done and keep the task on track.

Suggestions for connecting with directors:

Before meeting:

- Come prepared to be assertive and argue your points in the meetings. They do not appreciate weaknesses or too much doubt.
- Be ready to volunteer and take actions from their to-do list.
- Show willingness and allow space while they are expressing their thoughts.

During meeting (main goal is to stay focused on the task and getting things done):

- Be concise and stay on track.
- Show interest in the progress of plans/milestones.
- Listen to what they say and do not interrupt.
- Summarise/paraphrase their thinking.
- Emphasise actions, milestones, bottom-line impact/results, financial gains.
- Think things through – do not jump in.
- Do not invade their space.
- Demonstrate energy, commitment and passion to their agenda. Say yes a lot/be in agreement.

Words/sentences to connect with directors:

- 'In order to reach our targets, we should . . .'
- 'I think . . .'
- 'We are on track with our action plan . . .'
- 'The reasons for the lack of progress are . . . and we can mitigate these by . . .'
- 'I am happy to pick up this task for you' or 'So what you want me to do is . . .'
- 'I agree with you.'
- 'Our next steps are . . .'

How directors operate in a team:

- Get things done on time.
- Willingness to take risks.
- Ability to stay focused and resilient in the face of setbacks.
- Lead the group activity.
- Provide structure.
- Unblock problems and overcome obstacles.

What directors expect and need from their team to support them in getting things done. In relation to this, aim to:

- get to the point quickly
- be pragmatic/solution-focused
- pay more attention to the task rather than people

- help them deal with the emotional aspects of the task and how people are feeling
- give them information on how to 'read the room'
- understand that beneath the surface directors long to connect
- help them stop and reflect
- draw on the input and information of others
- challenge them when they are being unrealistic
- help them learn to rest, play, have fun and trust others.

Joe was a director type. After a debrief of his connector type, he realised that his continuous focus on the task damaged some of his relationships with team members. He decided to schedule regular one-to-one meetings in his diary to ensure that he listened to team members' concerns and inspirations. Feedback from team members was excellent. Joe's reputation has shifted to a leader who is capable of delivering sustained results as well as engaging staff and building high-performing teams.

EXERCISE

Try this today. Observe/shadow a director type for a meeting and analyse them using the following questions:

- *What did you notice about their body language, tone and presence?*
- *How did they participate in the meeting?*
- *What do they like or dislike? What do they find engaging? Are they blocking progress?*
- *Can you find your own director voice?*
- *How can you best work/relate with directors?*

What facilitators want:

- To facilitate the group and ensure commitment.

Suggestions for connecting with facilitators:

Before meeting:

- Be warm, unassuming and approachable.

- Show patience with their need to talk.
- Be ready to accept that it is worthwhile investing in getting people on board.

During meeting (main goal is to make sure that group harmony is maintained):

- Be optimistic.
- Show empathy and willingness to be open and express emotions.
- Emphasise loyalty, values, connections and wider societal goals.
- Keep eye contact and make sure that you are engaging the other person.
- Listen carefully and mirror their body language.
- Be sensitive to their emotions and show interest and curiosity.
- Show motivation to include everyone and aim for a participative approach/result.
- Ask for their opinions.

Words/sentences to connect with facilitators:

- 'I feel that . . .'
- 'It's an exciting opportunity.'
- 'We would love your input/contribution.'
- 'I value your experience/expertise in this area.'
- 'We want you to lead on this.'
- 'How do you think we should proceed?'
- 'Which people do you think we should involve?'
- 'This work will help emphasise social values' impact.'
- 'Joe and Suzan are involved. We are hoping that you can join too.'
- 'Morale is low and we think this project will increase engagement and harmony.'

How facilitators operate in a team:

- Excellent and loyal team members.
- Can read the emotions in the room and maintain team morale and engagement.

- Hard working and continuously work towards group decisions.
- Sense of fun, enjoyment, collaboration and encouragement.
- Sense of optimism.
- Maintain harmony and avoid unnecessary conflict.
- Enable others to reach higher goals.
- Interested in values, justice and social meaning.
- 'Social glue' not just the task, but also value the connections with team members.
- Networking with others.

What facilitators expect and need from their team in order to help maintain harmony. In relation to this, aim to:

- be involved and engage with them early on
- be open and honest with their views and feelings
- be positive
- help them address conflict, when appropriate
- help them with their tendency to please others and take on too much
- support with not getting over-emotional, and saying no/putting boundaries on others' requests
- coach them on how to be less sensitive/dependent on feedback from others.

Sheila was a facilitator type with a director connector boss. She felt that her boss wanted her to focus less on people/relationships and more on results. At times, her boss interrupted her in meetings and her contribution was being ignored. Having understood the gaps between the boss (director) and her (facilitator) types, Sheila began to pay more attention to how to connect to the boss's director type. She improved her conciseness in meetings, raised her energy and became more focused on outcomes. Sheila learnt to become less sensitive to her boss's critical comments. Over time, both her performance and the relationship with her boss improved.

What innovators want:

- To renew the group with new ideas.

Suggestions for connecting with innovators:

Before meeting:

- Show patience with their tendency to move from one thing to another.
- Have belief in their good intentions.
- Come ready to keep things open ended, and do not employ too much structure.
- Be prepared to be open/non-judgemental, and supportive of their ideas.
- Give them time to express their ideas.

During meeting (main goal is to ensure that there is space for discussing new ideas):

- Use expressive gestures.
- Be optimistic about what's possible.
- Show respect and listen to their ideas.
- Do not push for details and a great deal of planning.
- Excite them by offering new ideas/space for innovation.

Words/sentences to connect with innovators:

- 'I have an idea/concept.'
- 'Can you please tell me more about your idea/concept?'

- 'What can we do together?'
- 'It's exciting/inspirational.'

How innovators operate in a team:

- provide ideas outside the box and new information
- ensure that the group does not close too quickly on a course of action
- bring in the big picture, provide fresh thinking and energy.

What innovators expect and need from team members to help the generation of new ideas. In relation to this, aim to:

- provide innovation/new ideas
- add fresh/new perspectives/energy to the status quo
- create shortcuts and improve ways of working
- support and follow up with the details on their ideas
- respect and give space to their innovative and curious mind.

Ralph was an innovator type. He tended to jump from one project to another and struggled to follow up on actions. This gave an impression to other team members that he was not interested in collaborative working. Over time, he learnt to delegate some of the more mundane aspects of his work to junior members of the team. It helped him continue to innovate and perform without frustrating others.

EXERCISE

Try this today. Observe/shadow an innovator type for a meeting and analyse them using the following questions:

- *What did you notice about their body language, tone and presence?*
- *How did they participate in the meeting?*
- *What do they like or dislike? What do they find engaging? Are they blocking progress?*
- *Can you find your own innovator voice?*
- *How can you best work/relate with innovators?*

What specialists want:

- To support the group process with data and expertise, to improve quality.

Suggestions for connecting with specialists:

Before the meeting:

- Be prepared to be quiet and listen.
- Aim to be slightly more reserved and unassuming.
- Come to the meeting with your facts/data/evidence.
- Offer an agenda and an easy structure to follow.

During the meeting (main goal is to ensure that data/facts/knowledge are discussed in support of quality):

- Stay focused on the task and key points.
- Avoid personal and social chit chat.
- Explain things quietly and clearly.
- Emphasise quality and data.
- Show respect to specialists' professionalism/expertise.
- Use contained gestures.

Words/sentences to connect with specialists:

- 'I have worked in this area for X years and therefore believe.'
- 'In my professional view . . .'
- 'This paper/research/evidence suggests . . .'
- 'What's your expert view on this?'
- 'How about we look for more data/evidence?'
- 'How does this work impact quality?'

How specialists operate in a team:

- provide data and expertise to the decision-making process
- support with facts and evidence
- pay strong attention to detail
- ensure reliable and consistent delivery of projects.

What specialists expect and need team members to make sure that data/facts/knowledge are discussed, to improve quality. In relation to this, aim to:

- provide data/evidence/expertise to the task
- not be too loud
- avoid conflict
- be on point/concise/relevant and not take too much airtime
- be highly dependable
- ask them about their views and expertise
- challenge them to network with others
- involve them in strategic thinking
- help them deal with emotions and reading the room.

Richard was a specialist connector type. He wanted a promotion but, at the same time, found it difficult to network and navigate the organisational politics. His argument was that networking was a 'political/non-work activity' and he preferred people to judge his performance by expertise and bottom-line results. Over time, Richard realised the importance of nurturing strong relationships across the organisation to help him deliver complex projects. He learned how to get involved in a manner that suited his personality/energy and style.

EXERCISE

Try this today. Observe/shadow a specialist type for a meeting and analyse them using the following questions:

- *What did you notice about their body language, tone and presence?*
- *How did they participate in the meeting?*
- *What do they like or dislike? What do they find engaging? Are they blocking progress?*
- *Can you find your own specialist voice?*
- *How can you best work/relate with specialists?*

HOW DO DIFFERENT STYLES CLASH?

Owen (2018) argued that conflict between people with different connector types is healthy and part of any organisational life. Although we experience conflict as a threat to our core beliefs and self-worth, it should not necessarily be the case. If we handle conflict as an opportunity for learning and growth, we can learn more about ourselves and open up new opportunities for collaboration. Margaret Heffernan (2012) in her outstanding TED talk, 'Dare to disagree', argued that healthy conflict is the fuel for innovation and progress. She suggested that we need to give people tools to challenge authority appropriately and a set of principles on how to disagree well with each other.

We believe that the first step in handling conflict effectively is understanding some of the triggers for defensive behaviour and flexing your style accordingly. There are other useful things you can do when you are in conflict.

See the following tables for further elaboration/information on each type of conflict. There are no 'hard rules' in this area and we encourage you to experiment with these tips and learn from your experience.

Directors: conflicts and tensions with other styles (directors want to get the job done and view slowness negatively)

Triggers	Challenges	How to connect
Slow pace and reflection	Directors may find time to reflect both frustrating and challenging while other connector types may require space to articulate their thinking and consider options	Explain that you want to ensure we (team) get a quality result and want some time to consider all options. Give the director a deadline when you will be ready with answers and OK to proceed
Lack of decision making	Directors prefer quick decision making sometimes at the expense of taking risks. This preference goes against others who may want to engage more people and/ or require relevant data/ information before making a decision	Reassure directors that you are on their side and want progress that will satisfy all requirements. Show flexibility in areas where you can decide and move forward. Use a direct tone and fill in the silences

Triggers	Challenges	How to connect
Opening up agreed decisions	Directors favour closing quickly on decisions in order to progress and avoid ambiguity. They will experience opening up agreed decisions as both frustrating and stressful. Facilitators may want to open up agreed decisions, because they noticed that decisions are impacting negatively on harmony and morale. Innovators who are more relaxed about ambiguity may want to consider new innovative ideas that are suitable/ relevant	Explain the rationale for opening up the agreed decisions in a style that resonates with the director. Say 'We want to involve X so that we have her stronger support during the implementation phase.'
Discussion showing visible demonstration of emotions	Directors are oriented to dealing with tangibles such as plans, milestones, roles and responsibilities. They dislike the display of emotions that they perceive as irrational and getting in the way of progress	If possible, contain the display of emotions and reassure the director that you are on top of the task. Keep body language straight/focused and use concise language
Lack of progress	Directors want to get things done. Any delay/silences may be interpreted as lack of progress/not utilising time effectively. Others will be less concerned with lack of progress as their main preoccupation is new ideas and/or how people/morale are impacted	Show confidence, appear relaxed and fill in the silences. Reassure with ideas on how to put plans back on track

▶

Triggers	Challenges	How to connect
Low motivation/ willingness to take up responsibility and actions	Directors are high energy and want to achieve results with engaged people. Directors will struggle with people who are not motivated and reluctant to take up responsibility	Point out the team members who are showing interest and are willing to take up responsibility. Use directive words on what can be done. Show empathy with the director's frustration and offer new/practical ways to move forward
Too much 'politicking' and not enough action	Directors will view 'politicking' as something that does not contribute to the bottom line of the project	Offer to take from directors some of the 'politics'. Explain how this activity contributes to the project's progress. Frame 'politicking' as a positive activity that supports the completion of the task

Facilitators: conflicts and tensions with other styles (facilitators create harmony and view conflict negatively)

Triggers	Challenges	How to connect
People being highly directive and non-consultative	Facilitators are interested in teamwork and decision making. They will become stressed by a great deal of direction and lack of consultation	Listen sensitively to facilitators' concerns. If possible, reassure with a timetable of when team consultation will take place. Stay open, relaxed, curious about them and honest about your views
Being told what to do without explanation	Facilitators are motivated by a higher purpose/social meaning and values. They will experience lack of rationale for projects as stressful	Offer a participative process to co-create the rationale for the project. Listen to their criticism and, where possible, validate their perspective in an authentic manner

Triggers	Challenges	How to connect
People being assertive who are able to put down boundaries	Facilitators have a high need to please others and might feel slightly intimidated by people who can put down boundaries and say what they want	Explain the reasons behind putting down boundaries (e.g. self-care, other obligations) and reiterate your commitments to the wider social/values meaning and to them as human beings
Poor engagement/ ignoring individual and team contribution	This will hurt facilitators the most. Ignoring their contribution will be experienced as highly stressful	Stay calm, reassuring and explain that their contribution is extremely valuable. If you have a criticism, make sure you tackle specific behaviour/ input/topics rather than people/individuals
High pace/focus on the task with little space for reflection	Facilitators will experience this negatively. They like space for reflection	Make sure that you give them enough space to reflect and think with others. Signal that you value time and space for reflection. Also, emphasise that you value their contribution
Receiving critical feedback	Facilitators are highly sensitive to critical feedback	Make sure that you highlight the positives too. Remind them that you value their contribution. Do not be afraid to be human/emotional
Making a mistake	Facilitators may be worried that the mistake indicates lack of synergy with their values	To mitigate, apologise in an authentic way for any mistakes. Open up the possibility for a group conversation on what has happened and show willingness to discuss both contents and feelings arising from the mistake

▶

Innovators: conflicts and tensions with other styles (innovators make things better and dislike follow through and too much detail)

Triggers	Challenges	How to connect
Not considering their ideas	This will be highly stressful for innovators who are highly invested in their ideas	Explain that you are very interested in their ideas and book time in your diary to discuss. Show respect, match their pace/ enthusiasm
Too much detail in a meeting	Innovators will be stressed by focus on too much detail and can become bored quite easily	The best option is to refocus the meeting on the big ideas/dreams and ask other team members to follow up on the details. Keep the high pace and stay tuned to what is the overall thing they are trying to achieve
Heavy structure and mundane tasks	Innovators prefer an open-ended agenda to meetings. Heavy structure and mundane activities put them off	Try to add several agenda items that are more exciting. Allow for some free flow conversation at both the beginning and end of meetings. If you can, try to take away from them mundane tasks that can be better performed by other team members
Follow through/closure on actions	This does not play to their strengths and can trigger a great deal of anxiety	Stay calm and relaxed when they do not follow through on actions. Instead of becoming angry, hold in mind their other excellent input on innovation and change. Make sure that you listen and pay respect to their new ideas. When both of you are relaxed, choose two/three actions that require follow through and ask them to contribute

Triggers	Challenges	How to connect
Too much focus on quality	From the innovator's point of view, over-focus on quality may be experienced as annoying and over-detailed	Explain why quality is important. Listen to their ideas without interruptions. Help them see the importance of this aspect to their work, to customers and other key stakeholders
Not being able to innovate	This is the demise of every innovator	Look for an environment/ ways in which they can continue to innovate, grow and develop
Being asked to optimise/build from existing work	Innovators prefer to start things from scratch	Remind them of the value of optimising from existing products/knowledge/ relationships before rushing to the next new idea

Specialists: conflicts and tensions with other styles (specialists focus on the right decision for high quality, find it difficult to delegate and to handle ambiguous situations)

Triggers	Challenges	How to connect
Asked to perform 'small talk'/social chit chat/ network	Specialists value professionalism at work. They put a clear boundary between private life and work. Some may experience social interaction in the workplace as a bit awkward	Give them time, space and choice whether to participate and how to participate in a social activity. If you notice signs of anxiety, move quickly into the work agenda, which will be safer ground for them

Triggers	Challenges	How to connect
Delegating to others	Specialists' preference is to produce high-quality work and they find it difficult to delegate	Show the consequences of lack of delegation (e.g. over-work/burn-out, lack of team work). Encourage 'small experiments' with delegation of relatively minor issues and monitor progress. Offer for them to discuss delivery in team meetings. Review as a team how work is distributed, 'critical incidents', what's good enough and how to support each other
Discussion on general/ strategic questions	Specialists are more focused on their core expertise and details. They may find a strategic conversation more difficult/anxiety provoking	Give them time to prepare for a strategic meeting/ task. Praise them for positive contributions and trying out new behaviours outside their comfort zone
Being told that they are involved in too much data	Specialists are focused on details and may find it difficult if you challenge their style/pattern of getting soaked in too much analysis and data	Praise them for being detail-oriented and, at the same time, explain the overall vision and the importance of handling competing priorities. 'Good enough' is OK
Conversations with little data/evidence that has no relevance/ applicability	Specialists value data and practical ideas. They would look for these when interacting with you. Not having relevant data or providing ideas that are not practical will put them off and they will experience you as lacking in credibility	If you do not have the facts/data and/or practical ideas, acknowledge this and commit to searching for appropriate data/ evidence/practical solutions to support the conversation and next steps

Triggers	Challenges	How to connect
Being forced to a decision before they are ready/fast pace and insufficient time to think	This will be highly stressful for specialists	Give them time and space to reflect and offer ways to find out relevant information
Not taking into account their expert and professional advice	This is highly stressful for specialists	Reassure them of the importance of their expertise. Ask for their input/advice. Make sure you listen and integrate in the next steps. Talk softly and be friendly/unassuming
Show of emotions and high degree of conflict	Specialists put clear boundaries between private and work lives. They may fear emotions as being part of personal life/non-work	Try and minimise the level of visible emotion as much as possible. You can share feelings in a one-to-one setting and explore further
Context of ambiguity and change	Specialists have a desire for predictability and order. A degree of ambiguity can trigger stress	Seek and listen to their emotions/responses about the ambiguous context. To avoid paralysis, try and look for 'smaller'/concrete tasks so that they can move forward
Managing upwards	Specialists are bright and highly intelligent and some may not be aware of their impact on others. Therefore they can be less skilful in managing their 'boss'/upwards	Show empathy with some of their personal 'difficulties'/challenges to communicate and connect effectively, especially upwards. Show the consequences of their behaviours and offer ways to improve
Navigating complex and politically sensitive matters	Specialists are grounded in contents/data and will be uncomfortable in highly complex political situations	Guide/coach them on how to best tailor their messages. When needed, explain clearly some of the human sensitivities and complexities

▶

Triggers	Challenges	How to connect
Asking for them to rush the final product/ outcome at the expense of quality	Specialists do not like delivering poor-quality products	Acknowledge the dilemma between completing the task on time and quality. Show appreciation to the fact that they are willing to flex and go with 'good enough' product and quicker pace

---

EXERCISE

Improve your relationship with a key stakeholder

1. *First, identify yours and their connector type.*
2. *Think how to develop rapport using the section above.*
3. *Reflect on what you have tried to do in the past. What was the impact?*
4. *Which behaviours can you start to shift to enhance connection?*
5. *How do you feel about making these changes?*
6. *What are you learning?*

ADDRESSING INTERNAL CHALLENGES

As human beings, we are complex. Our personality is multi-faceted. It is normal to have a dominant connector as well as carry aspects of the other connector types. This can create some internal tensions and challenges. A director type may want to focus on the task but, at the same time, he/she has an influence from a less dominant facilitator type, which makes them aware that driving hard the task is impacting negatively on the morale and the relationships between team members. They feel caught between a rock and a hard place. In this situation, they need to learn how to adjust expectations on delivery so that they can give enough time/space for building a relationship with the team and taking account of varying levels of motivation. Another example is someone with a dominant specialist type with a keen interest in the quality of the product. She also possesses a strong but less dominant director type. She is experiencing a tension between her need for a high-quality product (specialist) and an obligation to deliver projects on time (director). Her strong specialist connector type means that she is attached to high-quality work and has difficulty delegating to others. Furthermore, she is less able to form relationships and has difficulty influencing others (low facilitator scores). Here, it is important for the specialist–director to have a discussion with others on what's a good enough product and reduce the pressure on high-end results to accommodate X's need for completion on time. Also, show the consequences of lack of delegation (e.g. overwork/burn-out, lack of team work). Encourage 'small experiments' with delegation of relatively safe/minor issues and monitor progress. Offer them to discuss delivery in team meetings and review as a team how work is distributed, 'critical incidents' of missing deadlines, what's good enough. Use email less and talk to each other, and team discussions on how to support each other.

Another common tension is between a director type (dominant) focused on a task who wants to get things done and a less dominant facilitator type who indicates that X is interested in creating harmony and pleasing others. Her strong director connector type means that X wants to deliver projects on time and, at times, loses empathy and patience with others. However, at the same time, X is torn as she is reluctant to drive the task too hard because of a less dominant yet important facilitator type that pushes her to 'please others' and avoid conflict with other team members. X is struggling to cope with this internal tension. In this scenario, it is vital for X to learn to manage her tendency to 'please others' by learning how to say no and trying small experiments of getting involved in difficult conversations/ conflict and learning from these experiences. In addition, X can delegate more work to team members and seek feedback on whether setting clearer boundaries with others was helpful or not.

EXERCISE

Your internal challenges

What are your dominant and less dominant connector types?

Try this today. Reflect on your personal pattern of connector types and implications of work:

1.

2.

3.

▶

Next week, try three new behaviours to address your internal conflicts (depending on your connector, see possible suggestions: delegate to others, speak up when needed, form relationships, reduce work load):

1.

2.

3.

SUMMARY AND ACTIONS

- Connector types complement each other.

- Having diverse types in your team/organisation improves your decision-making process and bottom-line results.

- Improved awareness of the needs, styles and triggers for stress in each type can help you create better relationships with others.

- Our personality is multi-faceted (e.g. we have at least two dominant connectors). It is important to pay attention to the internal challenges created by each unique combination on our well-being and performance.

Action plan for improving team connection and productivity:

- Ask your team to complete the online connector questionnaire using the enclosed link: https://public.virtual.ashridge.hult.edu/section/connector_type

  A hard copy is provided in the Appendix.

  Have a team conversation on the following:

- What is the individual connector style of each team member?

- What are our patterns as a team? Our emerging strengths as well as our developmental needs?

- In order to perform and communicate more effectively, what are our individual and group priorities for action?

CHAPTER 5

STRENGTHS AND OVERDONE STRENGTHS

Many of us will have to pass through the valley of the shadow again and again before we reach the mountaintops of our desires.

Jawaharlal Nehru

I n Chapter 2, we explored some of the implications for leaders in today's rapid pace of work environment. In order to solve complex organisational problems, leaders are required to utilise the diverse talents and experience of staff across the organisation. They need to create a psychologically safe environment for employees, so that they can speak up openly about the issues that are impacting them at work (Reitz & Higgins, 2019). Leaders are tasked with fostering collaboration across organisational boundaries. There is also a growing emphasis on the importance of increasing joy at work and decreasing burn-out. Against this backdrop, we have learned that leaders need to develop more relational capabilities and interact sensitively with others using both listening and humility. It is vital that they lead change in a less 'driven and hierarchical' way. Leaders need to employ their personality and experience, to get things done through their informal authority rather than positional power. Another implication is that leaders must be more self-critical of the impact of their behaviours on others. To help with this, we provided information in both Chapters 3 and 4 on the various connector types and how to communicate across connectors. We argued that being self-aware of your type and others will improve your ability to connect with others.

This chapter will give you the ability to:

- delve further into each connector type and explore how various connectors reach a state of 'flow', which happens when we are maximising our key strengths, focused on the task with clarity and confidence

- *understand what happens when you are pushing too hard and moving into the 'overdone strengths zone' and how to recognise when you are in the grip of this process*
- *apply coping strategies and tips on how to mitigate risks and avoid negative impact on yourself and others*
- *learn how to continue to nurture yourself as a leader, minimise the risks of 'overdone strengths' and ensure that you continue to be effective in the face of turbulent times.*

WHAT IS A STATE OF 'FLOW' AND HOW CAN YOU ACHIEVE IT AT WORK?

Csikszentmihalyi (2007), a psychologist and researcher into happiness, introduced the notion of state of 'flow' in activities such as art, play and work. He argued that 'flow' is when you are performing well in the context of a stretching challenge that is outside your normal comfort zone (though not in a way that it is beyond your capability). You can be with a friend, playing a musical instrument or in a meeting at work. What distinguishes the 'flow' state is that, despite the complexities, you are maximising your strengths and completely focused on the work. You have great inner clarity and confidence that you can do it. People who experience 'flow' say that time disappears and they feel as if they are part of a larger thing. Norman Augustine, former CEO of Lockheed Martin, said, 'Flow is about contributing something to the world and being happy while you do it.'

We argue that both 'flow'/maximising strengths and 'overdone strengths' are two sides of the same coin.

When we are in a 'state of flow', we are connected to ourself and others, working to our strengths and able to create effective and meaningful relationships. However, when we are not aware of our 'overdone strengths', we get distant from 'flow', struggle to connect and derail our key relationships.

However, let's first explore some of the key characteristics/behaviours of each type, which will help you achieve a state of 'flow' more frequently both at work and home. It will help you improve and sustain relationships, even when you are facing tough challenges.

Directors (want to get things done) are in 'flow' when:

- they are leading a high-performance team/project that is delivering to high standards
- they are initiating projects and making things happen

- they are moving at pace
- they are responding to changes quickly and overcoming obstacles.

Facilitators (create harmony with others) are in 'flow' when:

- they feel safe to speak up in a group
- they feel that people are treated well and collaborate respectfully with each other
- they can provide emotionally intelligent solutions to complex problems
- they are operating in harmonious teams with high levels of morale.

Innovators (make things better, improve) are in 'flow' when:

- their ideas are being considered seriously by others
- they are encouraged to come up with new ideas/concepts
- they are given the opportunity (time and space) to solve complex problems through creativity and 'outside the box' thinking.

Specialists (make the right decision for quality) are in 'flow' when:

- they can apply knowledge and expertise to technical problems
- they have clearer plans and a defined role within the project team
- they are contributing and producing high-quality outcomes
- they are part of an informative conversation that has data and evidence
- they see that others are both interested and impressed with their work.

EXERCISE

Try this today. What am I good at? What do I like doing (physical, mental, emotional)?

1.

2.

3.

Can you reflect on moments of 'flow' at work (e.g. highly challenged, maximising your skills and strengths, though not in a way that it is beyond your capability)? What were you doing? Who were you with? What factors helped you reach these moments of 'flow'?

▶

Can you think of three actions that you can implement to support you in having more of these 'moments'? (This is highly individual, but consider several examples: work with particular people, take time to relax/recover, try a new skill/hobby, prepare more for a presentation.)

1.

2.

3.

TOO MUCH OF A GOOD THING

Nevertheless, the state of 'flow' can become an overflow of good things. Strengths can derail us into 'overdone strengths' and lead to disappointments and poor performance.

Furnham (2013) claimed that leadership derailment is when a leader is unable to move forward: for example, being demoted or failing to reach a promotion; also, when the leader cannot adapt to the changing organisational context and/or believes that such adaptive behaviour is not in their range of capability.

Lombardo and Eichinger (1989) from the Center for Creative Leadership (CCL) in North Carolina offered further important research and examples in this area. They argued that many managers rely on their individual technical expertise to propel them into senior positions. However, as they are promoted, they fail to realise that the context demands them to develop the high-level relational skills that are vital for delivering tasks through others. As you start your career, being highly technical can be very helpful. However, if you continue to rely on these technical (cognitive) skills without the ability to form relationships, you are likely to derail (Gentry, 2016).

Similarly, key strengths can easily tip over to weaknesses, especially under stress. Confidence, which is an important trait for high-potential managers, over time can turn into over-confidence and arrogance. The ability to drive results can lead to over-ambition and pushiness. Sociability can become over-pleasing. Inspiration can turn into infallibility. Using knowledge too much can turn into lack of trust.

We provide below some of the typical overdone strengths for each connector type and tips on how to ensure continued and sustained high performance.

As a manager, being aware of these can help you to intervene effectively when one of your team members and/or direct reports is under-performing, due to moving into the danger zone of overdone strengths.

You will also be able to diffuse unnecessary interpersonal conflict and prevent personal derailment. You will become much more aware of both your individual strengths and overdone strengths, enabling you to improve your ability to form meaningful relationships, limit negative impact on others and fulfil your personal potential.

Overdone strengths of a director (wants to get things done)

Strengths	Overdone strengths
Focuses on goals	Single minded and lacking in empathy
Directs the team to achieve goals	Trusts others and delegates work
Keen on results	May appear critical of yourself and others
Task-oriented	May miss out on team and individual feelings
Highly confident	Can turn into arrogance

Overdone strengths of a director

Rosie was focused on getting things done. However, she was not able to delegate to others. She found it difficult to trust others, to perform even relatively non-complex tasks. Instead, she picked up too much work herself, resulting in lack of promotion and difficulties in her relationships at both work and home.

Overdone strengths of a facilitator (creates harmony with others)

Strengths	Overdone strengths
In tune with people's feelings	Can become over-sensitive
Sensitive to other people's feelings	Stressed by overreacting to others' emotions in an inappropriate way
Excellent team worker	Tries to rescue others, please others, struggles to put boundaries on others' requests, and say no
Seeks harmony and avoids unnecessary conflict	Can turn into avoiding crucial/courageous conversations
Reacts to emotions/feelings	Can be perceived as over-emotional/illogical

Overdone strengths of a facilitator

Ruben was experiencing difficulties leading his team. His empathetic/relational style created a good atmosphere within the team. Nevertheless, he tended to avoid conflict. This resulted in dysfunctional team performance, especially when tough decisions needed to be taken. Ruben wanted to please others and include everyone's opinions, which was impossible. He struggled to open a constructive dialogue on contested issues because he did not want to upset anyone. This cost Ruben his promotion.

Overdone strengths of an innovator (makes things better, improves)

Strengths	Overdone strengths
Moves from one creative idea to another	Struggles to follow through on actions
Preference for 'big picture'	May find details boring/less engaging
Curious mind that leads to improvement and innovation	Can get treble-booked
Likes to express their ideas	Many don't pay enough attention to others

Overdone strengths of an innovator

Zak was a senior executive. He tended to initiate many projects, but with little awareness of the extra demands/workload this created for others. He also failed to pay enough attention to budgets or to set realistic timelines for projects.

The outcome was that several projects got delayed. People were confused about their individual priorities. Through one-to-one coaching, Zak recruited a deputy who took charge of details, planning and resourcing. This remedial action avoided the executive derailing and ensured completion of projects on time, to budget and with a highly satisfied team.

Overdone strengths of a specialist (makes the right decision for quality)

Strengths	Overdone strengths
Focuses on individual area of expertise	Reluctant to contribute to wider strategy
Keen on quality of product	Can take too much time to complete tasks and may find it difficult to delegate
Prefers structure and detailed plan	Can become a hindrance when operating within ambiguous contexts
Introverted style is quiet and helpful in a team context	Can become an obstacle when more high energy/extroverted behaviour is needed, especially during conflict

Overdone strengths of a specialist

Jane was doing excellent work in her functional area and was considered for promotion. Her strength as a technical leader gained her a strong reputation in the business and credibility with senior management. However, when Jane was considered for promotion, she was viewed as 'too technical' and lacking in the level of interpersonal skills and political awareness needed to step up into a more senior role.

Lombardo and Eichinger (1989) argued that derailment of executives is costly and can be avoided. Individuals need to develop a checklist of their potential 'dark side', regularly review their progress and explore ways of mitigating risks. The section below will help you to do this.

'IN THE GRIP OF STRESS'

Kets de Vries (2006), a professor from INSEAD business school, argued that we carry around an 'inner theatre' of intimate relationships that we have struggled with throughout our childhood. Without being aware, we repeat the pattern of interactions with significant others in our childhood (e.g. parents, teachers). At times, this can unconsciously lead us into dysfunctional interactions with catastrophic outcomes. It can be triggered by a minor thing, such as a comment from someone, or an email.

One of the key challenges is to notice when our overdone strengths are being activated and we are hurting ourselves and others. Although it is not completely possible to avoid all the situations that may cause us to derail, it is advantageous to recognise the 'triggers' that push us from flow into overdone strengths.

See the table below, a checklist for noticing some of the hooks/stressors for each connector. These are sometimes difficult to recognise. At times, we may struggle to admit some of the personal 'weaknesses' to ourselves. In order to mitigate risks to the success of projects and loss of personal performance, it is important to understand our personal hooks and consider what can be done to overcome them.

Type	Hooks/stressors	'Antidote' to mitigate risks
Director (wants to get things done)	Low standards Hyper emotionality Failure to achieve goals Loss of control over quality, perceiving that there is too much time to think/reflect (silences) Slow response to emails Lack of ability to give robust feedback/input to issues	Give more time and space, 'let go' of your own agenda and listen to others Be less critical and supportive of others Listen and show empathy to the feelings of others

Type	Hooks/stressors	'Antidote' to mitigate risks
Facilitator (creates harmony with others)	Being described as selfish, being criticised and/or rejected. An environment of too much conflict Perceiving unfairness to others	Practise saying no Balance work/life demands, high stakes situations, practise detaching from emotions Become more 'selfish' and follow own agenda Make sure that you work on your pattern to 'rescue others' Be kind and generous to yourself
Innovator (makes things better/ improves)	Time to think Silence Details and plans Emphasis on deadlines Personal views that are not being considered	View details and planning as important and valuable Prepare agenda and follow through on actions Prioritise projects Recruit others to pick up/ follow up actions Show interest in others' projects
Specialist (makes the right decision for quality)	Small/social talk, broader issues, expertise being ignored Lack of planning and sudden/emergent change Low levels of expertise Low levels of quality	Ask someone in your network to have an informal coffee with you Bring a strategic topic to a meeting (e.g. communication strategy) Pay attention to the wider context of the project as well as social interaction Learn to live with ambiguity and, when possible, redefine your role and contribution

As demonstrated by the above table, the 'hooks' can be tricky for us to identify under pressure and require good levels of self-awareness. At times, we will need 'in the moment' feedback from others to help us notice when we are becoming driven by hooks. Losing sight of one's negative behaviours can damage your reputation and team performance. To help with this, see below some of the typical responses of each connector under stress and alternative replies, which are helpful to improve connection, communication and performance.

Typical responses by directors, triggered by stress and alternative responses

Typical response: 'I am busy.'

Alternative response: 'It's not personal but I am busy and can't help you right now.'

Typical response: 'Keep on working hard. We need to keep to the agreed timescales.'

Alternative responses: 'Shall we pause to review our behaviours and group process?'

'How do you/the team feel?'

Typical response: 'Who is responsible for this mistake?'

Alternative responses: 'What can we learn from this experience?'

'My mistake was . . .'

Typical response: 'You were late with your input. I am very upset.'

Alternative response: 'Is there any way I can support you to submit your report on time?'

Typical responses by facilitators, triggered by stress and alternative responses

Typical response: 'I am happy to help. When do you need me? I would love to help and am available Monday, Tuesday . . .'

Alternative responses: 'Let me check my diary to see when I am available.'

'Can you please tell me more about the project and why you need me?'

'I am currently busy but more than happy to help in the future.'

'It is not my role . . . but I know that X can help with this.'

Typical response: 'I feel overwhelmed and burdened by emotions from this situation. I am not sure what to do.'

Alternative responses: 'What is the data for what has actually happened?'

'What is a typical response to this kind of situation?'

Typical response by innovators, triggered by stress and alternative responses

Typical response: 'I love this idea . . . it can improve things so let's do it.'

Alternative responses: 'I am happy to help but need to check my diary. Is there someone else who can help with the next steps?'

'Who is going to help with the follow-up on actions?'

'What do you think?'

Typical responses by specialists, triggered by stress and alternative responses

Typical response: 'What do you think of my report? I used new models and data.'

Alternative response: 'Very good to see you. What did you do during the weekend?'

Typical response: 'Can you email me the information?'

Alternative response: 'Can we touch base for an informal coffee? I would like to hear your views.'

Typical response: 'It is not my role.'

Alternative response: 'Can you please say more about my contribution in this project?'

Typical response: 'Please do not distract me. I am focused on writing this report.'

Alternative response: 'I would like to know more. What is the general context for this project and how does this relate to my contribution?'

Typical response: 'The meeting was boring . . . too much conversation and high levels of emotions which was not professional.'

Alternative response: 'How did you feel about the meeting?'

EXERCISE

Mitigate the risks of your overdone strengths

In line with your connector type, try a remedial/antidote action next week.

- *What are you going to try (one of the alternative replies)?*
- *What was the impact?*
- *What will you change next time?*
- *How did you feel?*

There are several other important points to note:

- First, Tang (2019) argued that leaders should regularly conduct a mini audit (see above) on personal overdone strengths, as these can change over time. It is possible that something that may not have caused you any problems a few years ago is suddenly troubling you.
- Second, you may have worked hard and progressed on some of the factors that helped you to overcome difficulties. At the same time, the organisational climate has evolved, and your efforts may now need to be placed somewhere else.

Derailment can happen at an organisational level, too. See the example below:

CASE STUDY

The rise and fall of Nokia

Nokia was founded in Finland in 1865. Over the years, it was able to shift its core business from a manufacturing paper company to tyres and, since the 1970s, to world leader in electronics. In 1986, the company chose the mobile telephone as the first product to be marketed internationally under the brand name Nokia. It embarked on a highly successful acquisition strategy which resulted in outstanding financial results and sales. However, in the mid-2000s, Nokia was in a crisis. Commentators such as Doz and Kosonen (2008), who studied the organisational culture at Nokia during this period, argued that there was a loss of strategic agility at the top of the organisation. They were not able to make sense in real time of changes in the business environment, especially the growing demand for mobile phones. Doz and Kosonen related this to a subtle yet powerful change in the 'make up' of senior leadership. The visionaries who turned Nokia in the beginning of the 2000s were replaced by a group of managers who were highly professional and competent, but lacked both the strategic vision and agility of the previous generation of leaders. In the mid-2000s, senior management was oversensitive to numbers/performance at the stock market and lost sight of the importance of investing in R&D. This was one of the significant mistakes that led to the fall of Nokia.

There are several important lessons that can be drawn from the Nokia case study.

The new emerging generation of Nokia managers (mid-2000) was over-reliant on Nokia's success in the beginning of the 2000s. Confidence turned into arrogance. Also, the leadership of Nokia was not willing to explore the impact of the 'shadow side', of the overuse of key strengths.

The new generation of Nokia's managers were highly competent in their functional areas. However, this strength became a key weakness, as they lost sight of the key trends in the wider business landscape, resulting in slowness to invest in R&D and to mobilise resources in line with the changing market needs.

It is extremely valuable to assess the collective impact of the 'shadow side' of the leadership team of your organisation and associated risks. At the end of the chapter, we have designed a tailored exercise for your senior team. It will help them better understand what is currently working and what impact the 'shadow side' is having on the organisation.

SELF-HELP FOR LEADERS

At the outset of this chapter, we have already discussed why today's leaders require both toughness and high levels of self-awareness. Instead of the old-fashioned 'top down' approaches, they need to engage others through their personal leadership style, using participative methods. They are required to convene conversations across organisational silos, negotiate support for organisational changes, introduce insight and, when needed, have difficult conversations to improve both innovation and performance. The above is a tall order which puts a large amount of pressure on leaders.

Binney et al. (2009) argued that, instead of viewing leaders as 'superhuman beings', we should see them as 'ordinary heroes' who have three key roles; get real, get connected and get help. They claimed that the latter is the most critical. Receiving help is vital to ensuring sustained high performance and mitigating some of the risks of overdone strengths. We provide several exercises and information/tips on how to self-care. It will help you maintain your resilience and well-being during difficult times.

EXERCISE

My personal inventory

Reflecting on your career to date, note three experiences that you have dealt with well/effectively. What helped you? What did you do?

1.

2.

3.

What is my level of energy/resilience (1 low, 10 high)? *If you score lower than 6/7, see below for information/tips on how you can increase personal resilience.*

How do I take care of myself (1 low, 10 high)? *If you score lower than 6/7, see below for information and tips on how you can increase self-care.*

What is the quality of my social support (1 low, 10 high)? *If you score lower than 6/7, see below for information on how you can increase social support.*

To help with the above, we introduce pertinent research by Cooper et al. (2013) on four key areas that are critical to improving both personal and team resilience. We integrate this research and our experience into 10 practical tips to improve self-care and minimise the risks of overdone strengths.

Cooper et al. (2013) argued that the four key areas to improve your personal resilience are confidence, adaptability, social support and purposefulness (see figure below). They claimed that resilience is up to the individual and there are no easy answers. Each individual has to tailor his/her own solution. If we pay attention and integrate new behaviours, resilience can be improved over time.

In line with this, we would like you to choose from the menu of options and agree on actions right now that fit with your particular personality and work context.

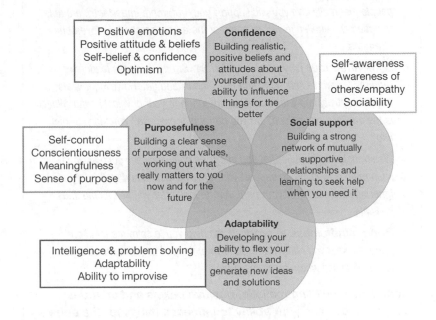

The four personal resilience resources
Source: Cooper et al., 2013

EXERCISE

Today, try this.

Adaptability (developing your ability to flex your approach and generate new ideas and solutions):

- *Ensure you receive robust regular feedback. No one likes (sometimes painful) feedback. We prefer to focus on our sunny/positive impact. However, in order to flex our range of leadership behaviours, it is vital to regularly consider our shadow and overdone strengths. When faced with unplanned change, do you stick with your old behaviours and patterns or do you adapt and try out new behaviours/skills?*

▶

We strongly recommend that you frequently seek 360-degree feedback from people working with you across the hierarchy, including line managers, peers and direct reports. Find out which of your leadership behaviours are working well. What should you stop doing? It's essential to ask for feedback from both supporters and critics. Remember the idea of tough love. The people that really love you will support you, but, more importantly, are able to notice and challenge you on some of the emerging shadows/overdone strengths.

- **Look after your physical condition.** Strong and agile leadership requires our whole self, including head, heart and gut. However, it is also a physical activity and you should pay attention to your physical health. What is the quality of your sleep? Do you do regular exercise? What is your diet like?

We strongly recommend that you integrate daily activities such as yoga, swimming or walking, to support your physical health and well-being. Ignoring your body is at your peril. Aim to look after yourself as much as possible.

- **Bring mindfulness to work.** It will help you to calm the mind and prioritise what you really want. Confront unhelpful negative thoughts and remain focused when the stress is high.

Confidence (building realistic, positive beliefs and attitudes about yourself and your ability to influence things for the better):

- **Hold a positive yet realistic view of yourself.** Confidence is key for successful leadership. Try to be both optimistic and realistic. This is a healthy tension. Continue to develop positive emotions within yourself and others. Confront over-critical and negative assumptions about your personal skills and abilities. Use reflection to identify natural strengths (see earlier 'personal inventory' exercise). Make sure that you stay positive, even when people around you are fearful and doubtful.

Next week, try this.

Social support (building a strong network of mutually supportive relationships and learning to seek help when you need it):

- **Expand and take care of your relationships.** We know that the quality of your networks is key to your effectiveness as a leader. It is part of your role to maintain engagement in social activity and have regular informal catch ups with your key stakeholders. Develop your emotional intelligence *and express gratitude for others whenever you can. Try this exercise: reflect on a recent successful project. Is there someone that you need to express gratitude to? Go and do it. What did you learn?*

- **Contain people's emotions, show vulnerability and seek help.** *Emotions are part of any change process. As people will naturally resist some of the changes being introduced, it is important that you can handle emotions such as blame, anger and envy. In parallel, make sure that, when needed, you are able to seek appropriate help from others. We believe that it's important to know the limits of our skills/experience and to look for advice from someone who can fill in the gaps. This will help you solve complex problems. Also, it will demonstrate to others that you are human. People prefer to connect better with people who show their vulnerabilities, not just their intellectual side. Jim Whitehurst, former CEO of open-source software maker Red Hat, has said, 'I found that being very open about the things I did not know actually had the opposite effect than I would have thought. It helped me build credibility.'*

Next month, try this:

- **Make sure you receive an external perspective on your performance.** *As you continue to grow into senior leadership, internal feedback on your performance is not enough. Many people will be aware of the internal politics and therefore may feel disempowered to speak up on the less effective aspects of your leadership. Here, it is vital to use external people (outside of your organisation) to test out your ideas and overall performance too. These can be confidants, supervisors and/or clients. Some of the questions you can consider asking include: How able am I to adapt to changing situations within a complex and multiple stakeholder environment? How am I relating to others under pressure? Do I have a compelling vision for my team/organisation?*

- **Practise humility and show concern to others.** *Be aware of flattery from others. It can trigger your hooks into the overdone strengths. Be humble and keep on praising others/the team for success. Zak published a study of Google employees which showed that managers who expressed interest and concern in other team members outperformed their colleagues in both the quality and quantity of their work (Zak, 2017).*

- **Learn from your mistakes and failures.** *Unfortunately, our progress in organisations depends on our successes. We are taught from early on in our careers that, in order to progress, we need to 'play the game' and*

▶

always show positive results. We marvel in our success. *However, our most profound learning and real confidence come from mistakes. Try and think of a recent failure. What did you learn?*

Purposefulness (building a clear sense of purpose and values, working out what really matters to you now and for the future):

- **Spend time thinking about what really matters to you.** *Set and pursue meaningful goals. We tend to define our success in a binary manner. We either won or lost the pitch/work. Our performance in the meeting was either good or bad. Our self-worth is wrapped in our last project. In the flurry of activities, we tend to forget connecting to the overall bigger purpose. Guy talked to an executive/administrator in a healthcare setting, who was continuously frustrated by the routine pressure of monitoring targets and performance. Over time, he lost sight of why he decided to work in healthcare in the first place. Following a coaching conversation, he started visiting the wards, seeing the terrific care for patients provided by his organisation, which was transforming people's lives. He became much more energised and able to deal with the relentless day-to-day activities by connecting to a wider goal.*

SUMMARY AND ACTIONS

- 'Flow'/maximising strengths and 'overdone strengths' are two sides of the same coin. Our strengths can become overdone strengths (too much of a good thing).
- Many managers rely on their individual technical expertise to propel them into senior positions. However, as they are promoted, they fail to realise that the context demands them to develop relational skills that are vital for delivering tasks through others.
- Under stress, we are more likely to rely on our overdone strengths. It can lead to low impact with others and, if these behaviours become persistent, to unnecessary interpersonal conflict and personal/career derailment.
- To avoid personal and organisational damage, it is important to receive regular robust feedback on personal performance/behaviours under pressure, identify triggers and seek appropriate support for yourself and from others.

Action plan for understanding the cumulative impact of your senior team (the question below is taken from Cooper et al., 2013):

■ List the top three qualities of the senior management team and the corresponding 'dark side'/overdone strengths.

Sunny side/strengths/qualities	Dark side/overdone strengths
1.	1.
2.	2.
3.	3.

■ What are your team strengths/qualities?
■ What is your collective 'shadow'/overdone strengths?
■ What are the implications for the senior team and the wider organisation?

PART II

'RESOLVE' MODEL OF CONNECTING

CHAPTER 6

THE RESOLVE MODEL OF CONNECTION

Peace is not the absence of conflict, but the ability to cope with it.

Mahatma Gandhi

RESOLVE is a model designed to manage conflict instead of letting the conflict manage you. People are afraid of conflicts because, by definition, they are uncomfortable. This results in trying to avoid them as much as possible. The track record of the avoidance route is poor. Unresolved conflicts lead to strained communication, difficulties in teamwork, decreased productivity, higher turnover and a toxic work environment. Our experience is that conflicts, if managed wisely, are, in fact, huge opportunities to strengthen relationships. This chapter provides tools that will give you confidence to deal with conflicts and discover their potential in terms of building trust, enhancing creativity and opening the doors to new practices.

This chapter will give you the ability to:

- build the necessary skills to resolve conflicts and turn stressful situations into empowering moments
- connect to others' perspectives in a way that benefits all stakeholders
- establish boundaries and identify what is actually important
- choose your battles wisely in a way that will maximise gain and reduce unnecessary losses
- act from your power zone by distinguishing what is real and what isn't and knowing what you can change and what you cannot
- assess timing and have confidence about when to act and when to wait
- link RESOLVE to how it can be used by people with different connector types.

When solving problems, dig at the roots instead of just hacking at the leaves.

Anthony J. D'Angelo

RESOLVE presents seven tools for resolving stressful situations and addressing conflict. Having practical tools to manage conflict will help you manage difficult situations in a way that will create an open and productive dialogue. This will bolster your internal clarity about your goals and intentions, which, in turn, will translate to external confidence. People around you will trust you because complex issues won't be swept under the rug, but will be used to create a thriving and open-dialogue work environment.

The process of resolving conflicts does not guarantee a life without problems. It is a process in which you will have both small wins and major setbacks. The true potential of conflicts is hidden in the process of resolving them. While we wish we could promise that the other side will immediately see the light, realising how wrong they were, and engage in intense, loving acts of repair, that unfortunately is not a realistic expectation. The process of resolving a conflict requires a constant negotiation, give and take and compromise. The outcome is likely to be different from what you envisioned it would be. It is important to keep that expectation in your mind during any conflict resolution process.

Ready to give it a try?

It is especially effective to read about the tools *while keeping in mind* a current and relevant conflict.

RESOLVE MODEL AT A GLANCE

Realise reality: find clarity in situations and focus on issues that are actually under your control.

Establish clear boundaries: negotiate with clarity and confidence about what is important to you and what are your red lines.

Seek support: elicit the right kind of support because, more often than not, it helps to have at least one person on your side.

Own your part: have the courage to say, 'I am sorry' when and where appropriate and acknowledge your strengths as well as your shortcomings.

Listen: open the door to improving your listening skills.

Validate and agree: remember the power of seeing, hearing and understanding someone else's perspective.

Evolve: focus on timing, especially knowing the right time to act.

The model is not linear. It outlines seven different tools that can help you address conflict effectively. The final tool, *Evolve*, will help you to assess where you are, what the situation requires, and what the best next path forward is.

There are multiple options and approaches for using the RESOLVE model. You can read it all or cherry pick the tools you need. The most important element of this model is that you play around with it, tailor it to specifically meet your particular needs, and make it yours.

TOOL # 1: REALISE REALITY

> *When your mind is racing, you feel your clarity was stolen by a hurricane of emotions and things seem to be out of control. This means that it is time to refocus by connecting to what is real and is effectively under your control.*

The first tool in this process requires us to engage in an internal examination of ourselves, defining what is and what isn't real, as well as what is and what isn't under our control. Being able to distinguish between reality and fantasy can save you from the anxiety of chasing imaginary demons or wild fantasies. While it may sound simple, organising your thinking is paramount to making informed decisions and taking effective actions. We name the space where things are real and under our control our *power zone* because, when you act from this place, intentions turn to outcomes.

What is real?

The majority of conflicts take place inside our minds. In a tweet from *Psychology Today*, Dr Leslie Becker-Phelps (2019) states: 'Don't believe everything you think', and adds that 'learning to separate your thoughts and beliefs can change your life'.

The 'monster moment' shown below is an excellent example of the ways our thinking can mislead us and create unnecessary battles:

- Josh's story is an example of a grown-up version of our childhood 'monster moments'. Just like a child in the middle of the night who is terrified of a monster, our adult 'monster moments' come from a combination of fear and the unknown. These fears can grow and, if left unchecked, can create a fictitious story based on false assumptions. These assumptions may spiral out of control and create a 'monster' in your mind. Most conflicts are created from a monster story similar to this.

CASE STUDY

Josh

Josh is a youngish, mid-level manager in a medium-sized non-profit organisation. He manages 15 employees who are all older and have more work experience than he does. In the last few years, he has been promoted several times and moved up the corporate ladder faster than most of his peers. He also has been in therapy because he has constant feelings that some of his team members are trying to 'get rid' of him and that they have complained to senior management about the way he manages and the decisions he makes.

Shortly after his first two therapy sessions, he called and requested an 'emergency appointment' with his therapist. He came to the appointment with three versions of a resignation letter, all of which would pre-empt what he saw as a definite termination coming soon. He lamented that 'everybody is treating me differently', and that a board member, working with him on a quality assurance community report, did not reply to several of his recent emails. He relayed that, at the last board meeting, the board called for an executive session to which he was not invited. He felt strongly that all the evidence pointed to the fact they were going to fire him.

His therapist suggested that he put any resignation process on hold, and together they would consider a 'reality test'. With his therapist, Josh identified a board member with whom he had a good working relationship. When back in the office, Josh reached out and scheduled a meeting with the board member. Josh took the risk of talking with this board member about his concerns. At the meeting, Josh learned that the executive session was indeed about him: the board had been discussing a raise for him to reward his hard work and had voted, unanimously, to approve it. The treasurer had been tasked with a budget review in order to see how much they could offer him!

After processing this news and his false beliefs, Josh then took another risk, sharing this story with his team, talking about his concerns of what, in his mind, was his insecurity of seeming less experienced due to his age. They were surprised, stating that they loved his passion and humility and, since then, Josh and his team use the phrase, 'I had a "monster moment"'.

Josh is not unique. We all have our own daily 'monster moments'. The way to deal with these is to shed light on them and be aware of our false assumptions.

Monster moments are powerful and convincing but, nevertheless, they are not real. They minimise your ability to see the situation for what it is and address it effectively. In order to deal with those moments, you need to shed light upon them.

EXERCISE

What to do when you have identified a 'monster moment'

Identify your basic assumptions regarding this situation (e.g. I am not good enough, this cannot be resolved, the 'other side' does not want to collaborate, I cannot trust anyone).

Once you have identified these basic assumptions, you are already ahead of the game because you are ready to look under the bed and discover if there is or isn't a monster hiding there. You have shed light upon the assumption that might have prevented you from moving forward. You can try any one of the following approaches:

1. *Turn any assumption into a question. (Am I good enough? Can I trust this person? Is the other side willing to collaborate?) Think what would be different if the answer is 'yes' (e.g. I am good enough! I can trust this person. The other side is willing to collaborate.). Then see if there is any action you can take in order to challenge your basic assumption. You could ask for a reality check. It could sound something like this: 'My assumption is that you are not interested in collaborating, but I am not sure I am right about that. I need a reality check. How do you feel?' We are aware that doing something like this feels risky. Our experience is that it is an effective way to approach others.*

2. *Put yourself in the place of other stakeholders: what would they say? What do they feel? Why are they behaving the way they do? This can be challenging to our psyche, but it is always beneficial. If you have a group of friends whom you feel comfortable asking for candid feedback from their perspective, this is a valuable resource to utilise. Ask a trusted friend or colleague if they are willing to listen to your conflict and provide you with an honest different perspective. Be prepared and open to hearing something that does not back up your perspective.*

What is under your control?

If you want to go the extra mile, we recommend examining whether something is under your control or not. The famous 'Serenity Prayer', the common name for a *prayer* written by American theologian Reinhold Niebuhr, states:

> *God grant me the serenity to accept the things I cannot*
> *change, courage to change the things I can, and wisdom*
> *to know the difference.*

We can determine what is (and what is not) under our control by using a simple test:

- *Yes:* if I can do something about it, it is under my control.
- *No:* if I cannot do anything about it, then, atleast right now, it is not under my control.

No matter how hard we try and, despite our best efforts, we cannot make the sun rise from the West, we cannot stop the rain, and we cannot control earthquakes, floods, etc. In the same way, we cannot control how other people think, feel or behave – though we often believe we can. On the other hand, we *can* make choices about *how we deal with* the sun rising, the rain falling, or an earthquake occurring. In difficult and conflictual situations, there is a natural tendency to attempt to manage things that are not under our control, like managing others' actions and behaviours. Distinguishing between what is under your control and what isn't will help you gain clarity and prevent loss of time and other resources.

EXERCISE

Focus on what is under your control

Think about a stressful situation you are, or have been, in and make a list of things that are, and are not, under your control in this scenario.

Under your control	Not under your control
Examples:	Examples:
I can write an email explaining my situation	The decisions made by senior management and the board

▶

Under your control	Not under your control
I can control the way my team would address this challenge	The fact that they do not want to approve my plan
I can commit to do my best to resolve this situation	The overall company budget
I can ask certain people for advice	The political environment
	The company culture
	Other people's moods, actions and life problems

Oftentimes, simply acknowledging what is real and under your control propels you into a powerful position, allowing you to move forward with clarity and confidence, feeling connected and empowered.

TOOL # 2: ESTABLISH CLEAR BOUNDARIES

> *Winds of conflict can carry you far from what is really important to you. You may find yourself fighting for things that you are not really interested in, while neglecting what you value. Connecting to what is significant to you is coming back home to things that are truly meaningful in your work and in your life.*

When we fail to set boundaries and hold people accountable, we feel used and mistreated.

Brené Brown

This tool focuses on establishing boundaries. Boundaries represent your personal space and what you consider yours; your material belongings as well as your values, opinions, ideas and preferences. Within your boundaries, you feel at home, safe and comfortable. Conflict resolution and any negotiation require exploration outside the safety of your home, outside of your comfort zone.

One of the managers we worked with explained it as follows: 'Dealing with everyday conflicts in the office, I know I will have to learn to do things differently, but, at the end of the day, I still want to recognise the person that I see in the mirror. I want to know that I was flexible and accommodating while protecting fiercely what is vital to me. This means that every day I need to remind myself what is essential, so I won't engage in unnecessary battles and I also won't violate my values and principles.

The process of conflict resolution is based on a 'give and take'. It is a delicate balancing act; you need to be flexible enough in order to accommodate someone else's wants and needs, yet firm enough to respect and not cross your own boundaries.

Relationships can be assessed by looking at the balance of this 'give and take' harmony. Your job is to know exactly what you are willing to give, what is negotiable and what is not, and what constitutes a radical and firm 'no' from you. As long as you don't violate your own boundaries by neglecting what is important to you, you are free to engage in the negotiation process. Let's say you prioritise being home with the family and having a healthy work–life balance, then working extra hours in the office instead of playing with your children would be a 'no go', regardless of consequences. You might, in this case, offer to be effective in another way. While this process may push you outside your comfort zone, it will also allow you to explore new terrain. It is difficult to be truly flexible when you don't have a solid foundation to come back to. This foundation includes being aware of your core values, needs and wants.

EXERCISE

Establish clear boundaries

When you are not aware of your values, your foundation is weak, and the base you have built it upon is not stable.

Define your values:

What are your personal values (e.g. balance, freedom, beauty, family, community, achievement, recognition, security, health, wealth, service, peace, love, justice)? Choose three values that are the most important to you:

1.

2.

3.

Then focus on a specific situation and define:

What do you need? (Things that are essential, that are unnegotiable.)

1.

2.

3.

What do you want?

1.

2.

3.

What is negotiable? Identify the areas you are willing to negotiate on (or what you are willing to give).

1.

2.

3.

The following diagram illustrates how a boundary-based conflict resolution works.

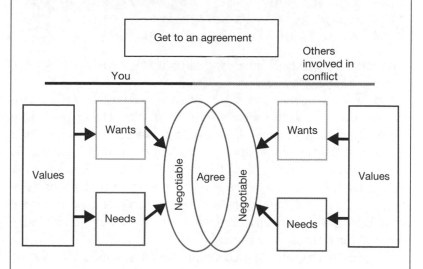

Conducting value-based dialogues tends to be effective because it is based on the core of what is important to all sides involved in the conflict. Adding to it clarity of needs and wants, makes it much easier to achieve your goals, and has the potential to foster a supportive environment that enables solutions.

This clarity can allow you to use the following question that may bring about much-needed clarity.

Fill in the blanks below for your own particular situation.

Open the lock question:

'I need/want _____. What do you need/want in order for _____ to happen?'

Once our goals are clear, we are both able and willing to accommodate the other side's needs. We are already well on our way to resolving many conflicts!

TOOL # 3: SEEK SUPPORT

> *Gain the courage to reach out, acknowledging you need help, and get the support that will help you resolve your problem.*

Support is the biggest investment you can make in your life. A little bit of it can make a huge difference.

Support is the cornerstone of our existence. Having personal and professional supportive relationships are a solid predictor of health, well-being and success. Emmy Werner and Ruth Smith, researchers in the Kauai Longitudinal Study (Werner, 2005), found that children who grew up in impoverished and challenging situations were able to become functional and successful adults if they had a 'supportive relationship with at least one reliable adult'. In the same way, having one good, reliable co-worker friend can help transform your entire working experience, making you resilient – even in a dysfunctional environment.

Once you are involved in a conflict, it can be extremely important to activate your support network. In order to do this, you should have your support network built and ready to go, even if just for that. Relatively few working professionals find it easy to ask for help when needed, many more prefer not to do it, being concerned about revealing weaknesses and/or vulnerabilities.

Dig deeper; ask yourself: how easy it is for you to seek support?

Look at the 10 questions written below. Be candid with yourself and check on how many of them you can honestly answer positively. Each one of these is a tool for increasing resilience. You do not need to adapt them all, of course, but you can choose to work with ones that suit you. You will be able to feel the results quite quickly.

Enter *yes*, *no* or *partly* in the table below.

1.	Do you spend as much time as you possibly can with people who care about you and in whom you feel empowered in their presence?	
2.	Do you ask for help when needed? (See more about seeking help in the next paragraph.)	
3.	Do you work to build stable routines and habits?	

4.	Do you engage in mindful practices, like meditation, yoga and relaxation techniques?	
5.	Do you exercise regularly?	
6.	Do you spend time and effort to build a sense of mastery in your work?	
7.	Do you leave time to play, i.e. enjoy lightness and levity in your life?	
8.	Do you actively express gratitude?	
9.	Are you generous with yourself and others?	
10.	Did you, or do you cultivate a sense of humour? (Yes, humour is a skill that can be developed!)	

Examine your answers: how many *yes's* did you enter above? Any place you marked *no*, or *partly*, needs your attention and a decision if there is anything you would want to do about it.

As our years of experience in working with executives in leadership positions indicates, the reluctance to seek support is rather frequent. It is exacerbated by an antiquated view that celebrates 'the lone wolf' and heroic leaders who have all the answers. Instead of searching for help or assistance, many leaders tend to hide behind a facade of certainty and false confidence, pretending that everything is cool and under control.

TOOL # 4: OWN IT!

Move beyond the confinement of knowing what everybody else did wrong. Realising your contribution to the specific situation, for better and worse, should yield better outcomes in terms of your ability to resolve conflicts.

Knowing yourself is the beginning of all wisdom.

Aristotle

Sun Tzu in *The Art of War* (Giles, 2013) wisely pointed out that, 'If you know the enemy and know yourself, you need not fear the results of a hundred battles. If you know yourself but not the enemy, for every victory gained, you will also suffer a defeat. If you know neither the enemy nor yourself, you will succumb in every battle.'

It's a tall order, knowing yourself intimately. It requires recognising your strengths, weaknesses, limiting beliefs and vulnerabilities. Acknowledging and facing your fears – a difficult step – can seem as if it borders on the impossible, as there will always be aspects of ourselves, others and situations that are unknown to us. The goal is to strive to know as much as possible.

Owning our strengths

The next step is to understand your strengths and acknowledge what you bring to the table. Contributing is a key feature in our human existence – we need to be and feel effective.

In her book, *A Return to Love* (1992), Marianne Williamson wrote:

> *Our deepest fear is not that we are inadequate.*
>
> *Our deepest fear is that we are powerful beyond measure.*
>
> *It is our light, not our darkness*
>
> *That most frightens us.*

EXERCISE

Take time to focus on your strengths and contribution to the relevant situation

My biggest contributions to this project, company, event, etc. are:

1.

2.

3.

4.

5.

How can my strengths contribute to resolving the conflict?

1.

2.

3.

4.

Unveiling our shadow: weaknesses, limiting beliefs and vulnerabilities

You either walk inside your story and own it or you stand outside your story and hustle for your worthiness.

Brené Brown

An interesting concept about unveiling our shadow is that we all share the same basic vulnerability. Most of us deny the fact that we feel inadequate in some aspect of our lives, that we are not good enough, incompetent and that others would discover that we are just pretending.

Owning our fears

Fear is a big factor in the way we live and a major contributor to conflicts. Facing our fears, examining them closely, admitting them and working with them is a major part of any resolution.

Fear and anxiety are future-oriented. We all share the same fundamental fear: *loss*. We fear losing control, losing our health, losing meaning, losing family members and friends, losing others' appreciation and respect, losing our voice, losing the ability to be effective, losing career and professional reputation and, of course, losing our lives. The two most prominent fears that we all have (and try to hide) are the fear of not being good enough and the fear of not being loved.

Managing your fears takes time because we need to open a dialogue with them, acknowledging them, inviting them in, trying to determine their origin and listening to the story they want to tell. This exercise involves going the extra mile and takes practice, but it is worthwhile.

To many of you, this may sound impossible or uncomfortable because most of our workplaces don't encourage – or even allow – this kind of candid and direct interaction. Just imagine how much more authentic your life would be if you could comfortably say: 'I am sorry I was rude to you. I was afraid that we wouldn't finish this project on time.' While it would make our lives immeasurably easier, as a culture, we are not at a place where direct candour is comfortable. The obvious starting point is taking the next baby step towards acknowledging our fears internally.

TOOL # 5: LISTEN

When engaged in a conflict, especially if it's around something important to you, your ability to listen may be compromised. This tool is about mastering the art of listening.

Wisdom is the reward you get for a lifetime of listening when you'd have preferred to talk.

Doug Larson

Listening is a powerful tool in relationships. It has the power to transform conflicts to solutions and foes into friends. Renowned author Stephen Covey argued that, 'most people do not listen with the intent to understand; they listen with the intent to reply' (Covey, 2005). In 2015, the *Harvard Business Review (HBR)* announced Lars Sørensen, CEO of Novo Nordisk, as the best CEO for the second year running. Judges from *HBR* explained that this was based on exceptional delivery of business results and Sørensen's ability to work collaboratively with his management team and scientists across the business. His humility, collaborative style, courage to seek advice/help from others, and ability to listen and implement were praised as outstanding and the key for both individual and organisational success. Sørensen was able to lead experts without understanding their field because he was able to truly listen to them.

The act of listening is both an intention and a skill. It entails the intention of truly hearing and understanding someone else, and it requires openness, curiosity and purposefully avoiding the temptation of taking the content personally, or trying to fix the other person. When you make an honest attempt to understand someone else, it increases significantly the chances that this person will be open to you and, even if they don't, the attempt to understand already makes a difference. True listening opens the door to creativity, deeper understanding and a sincere willingness to accommodate others' needs and requests.

One reason that we don't benefit from the power of listening is that we often stumble upon obstacles, closing our ears and blocking our hearts.

These are some of the most common *obstacles*:

- The fear of being wrong (prevalent with people with a dominant specialist connector type).
- Being hijacked by emotions that may get stirred up during the conversation (prevalent with people with a dominant facilitator connector type).
- The need to perform, sound knowledgeable and smart (prevalent with people with a dominant specialist connector type).
- The need to 'fix' the other person or issues at hand (prevalent with people with a dominant director connector type).
- Being distracted, most often by our phones or other technology (read: rude!) (prevalent with people with a dominant innovator connector type).

After removing these obstacles, the next step is to put ourselves in a frame of mind of being genuinely curious about where the other person is coming from. By setting a clear and mindful intention to fully listen, you will discover a whole new world and a whole new person and, if your main objective is to fully understand the other person, the quality of your interaction will change. You will naturally ask more questions and, in turn, be careful to verify that you actually understood the other person.

Every communication between individuals contains thousands of signals. The signals are sent and received on different levels: physical, emotional and mental. There are signals on the content level which contains the words that are expressed, there are signals of unspoken messages underneath the words also known as sub-text, there are signals on the emotional level, and there are signals on the level that represents what I want from you and what I think you want from me. It is a lot and it is complex. If listening is one of your challenges, we highly recommend that you learn more about it, read a book, practise and elicit feedback.

Listening exercise

Choose an important conversation. Commit to listening with the purpose of understanding. Before you reply, verify that you have fully understood the content. Summarise the content you just heard and verify it by asking: 'Did I get that right?' Then, ask if there is anything else that he or she needs to add for further clarification. Respond only after being completely convinced that you fully understood what the other person wanted to express.

The following question can go a long way towards resolving conflicts: 'I need or want _____ because of _____. What do you need in order to make this happen?'

Then *simply listen with the purpose of understanding the other person's response.* If what you want is completely unacceptable to the other person, ask questions to understand why. You should then allow the other person's perspective to reshape. Conventional wisdom traditionally held that the most important aspect of all relationships was communication. However, we now understand that relationships depend not only on our willingness to listen, *but also on our ability to shift our perspective and to be influenced by what we hear.*

TOOL # 6: VALIDATE

> *I see you, I hear you and I understand . . . so how can we move forward together?*

Validation can calm the storm of emotions, de-escalating almost any situation. This involves going beyond listening to the other person – it requires understanding where they are coming from, seeing the situation through their eyes, and walking for a moment in their proverbial shoes. The act of validation opens the door to honest communication because it *disarms* us. Something shifts inside when we feel heard and understood. On her final show (25 May 2011), Oprah Winfrey shared the most important lessons she learned after interviewing nearly 30,000 guests. She stated that all the people she talked to had one thing in common: *they wanted to be validated*. In her words: 'Every single person you will ever meet shares that common desire. They want to know: "Do you see me? Do you hear me? Does what I say mean anything to you?"'

McKay, Davis and Fanning (2009) devoted an entire chapter of their book to validation, explaining that 'validation is a powerful tool that can be used in any situation where there is a real or potential conflict'. In conflict, emotions run high and our ability to use our cognitive ability declines as the fight or flight dynamic takes over, blocking us from thinking clearly.

When we are triggered, it is hard – almost impossible – to see or understand someone else. The first step towards trying to understand another is always to reconnect internally and finding why we are blocked from connecting to someone else. Once we recognise that we've been triggered, we can say to ourselves, 'Right now, I have been triggered. I don't know what to do about it. It is OK, and I can wait until I gain more understanding of the situation.'

When we have achieved some clarity, we can devote some mental resources to see, hear and connect with someone else. Remember, validating does not mean agreeing; it means that '*I see you, I hear you and I can relate to you*'.

TOOL # 7: EVOLVE

> *When it all comes together: Evolve or Dissolve.*

The goal of the first six tools is to open a space where you can function beyond the flight, fight and freeze natural response instincts. Being able to realise your 'monster moments', know what your values are, and articulate these values is essential. Having enough support from your network and honing the skills of listening and validation will allow you to make informed decisions. Now, when you are centred and self-aware, you are faced with a crucial decision: are you going to proceed with this process or resign?

If you decide to proceed and stay engaged in resolving a conflict, it would be wise to create a risk assessment first. Great gains often involve great risks. The risk needs to be calculated so that it can be judged as being worth the risk.

Green

Green is when we have a partner involved in the conflict who is engaged and provides the safety to express ourselves directly. If this is the case, you should communicate with the other stakeholders verbally or in writing the following:

- What is important to you?
- What you do truly appreciate about them?
- What you do need from them?
- And what are you willing to provide for them (if you know this)?

This would lead you to the final and most important question for your stakeholder, which is:

- *What is really important to you?*

And then truly listen to this person respond to that question. Once you know what your own boundaries are, chances are that you will surprise yourself with your new confidence on this topic and by how much easier it is to truly listen to and understand what others have to say about what is important to them.

Yellow

This phase is when you are not sure if your stakeholders are open and willing to listen and meet you in a negotiation space. This is the 'unknown' stage. It may feel risky to approach them for further negotiation. This phase requires more information enquiring about what is important to them:

- What are their values?
- What is important to them?
- How can you communicate with them?
- What is the best way to approach them?

Solicit information in a sort of 'background check'. Learning about them in the light of this new information will let you know if it is a red or green situation.

Red

This stage is when you and your stakeholders feel like there is no possible open door for further dialogue. You assess that it is too risky to approach them for a meeting around the table.

This calls for these actions:

■ Find a connector from your support network who can help you access the stakeholders.

■ Send an impartial person who can approach the stakeholder calmly and productively.

The ultimate goal here is to employ this connector to get you and the stakeholder in question to a table for a conversation around the issue. That is, to get to 'green'.

Proceed with the following exercise for your conflict's risk assessment. The system to calculate the risk calls for the 'green, yellow and red system'.

The way to determine where you are can be intuitive. You can know if you are in the green zone and negotiating is a *go*, or you are in the yellow zone and it is time to *wait* and gather more information, or you are in the red zone, which means *stop*. You can use the following chart in order to define if you are in green, yellow, or red:

Answer the following by rating yourself on a scale from 1 to 10 (1 is low, and 10 is high):

You trust yourself to be able to handle the negotiation process	
You trust that the other stakeholder's intention is to find an acceptable solution	
You can imagine or see a solution that would be acceptable to all stakeholders	
You feel that you are able to manage your stress in a productive way	
You have enough support which allows you to deal with less than optimal outcomes	
Total score	

Green light: if you rated yourself above 5 in all categories and your overall score is higher than 40.

Yellow light: you don't have any score that is below 2 and your overall score is between 20–40.

Red light: you have one score or more under 2 *or* your score is under 20.

RESOLVE AND CONNECTOR TYPES

The last section deals with the four connector types: director, facilitator, innovator and specialist. We all have a dominant connector type that governs the way we understand the world and the way we act in it. Our connector type also reveals our patterns in resolving conflicts. Each connector type has strength and weakness in implementing the RESOLVE.

Find your dominant connector type (there is more on this in Chapter 3).

Connector type	RESOLVE strengths	RESOLVE challenges	Remedies
Director	Has a natural ability to own strength and weakness Is not afraid to say: 'I am sorry' and build an effective team that will compensate for their areas of weakness Usually has the confidence and ability to identify what is real	Known for being rigid and lacks the flexibility needed in order to compromise Has difficulty asking for help or delegating Avoids conflicts and has a tendency to find it difficult managing emotional situations	Learn to be vulnerable and ask for help Practise listening skills and increase ability to be flexible Engage in playful activities where you can practise seeing situations from different perspectives and be more spontaneous
Facilitator	Has a gift in listening to others and validating Known as being supportive and able to create harmonious working environments	Experiences difficulties in setting boundaries and owning strengths Tends to avoid conflict because of the fear of hurting others and the need to 'live in harmony'	Learn to be more assertive Understand that setting boundaries is a kind act because it helps guide people through challenging situations Accept the fact that they deserve to be supported

▶

Connector type	RESOLVE strengths	RESOLVE challenges	Remedies
Innovator	Has the tendency to be flexible and creative in terms of finding innovating ideas Can connect to people and validate	Has the tendency to be distracted and not consistent Has difficulty accepting structures and boundaries Lacks consistency and reliability that makes it challenging for people with other dominant connector types Avoids conflict by having an 'idea' that bypasses the real problems	Be consistent and focused Accept help from directors and specialists in order to stay on track and follow through on actions Learn to compromise and give space to ideas initiated by others
Specialist	Tends to be methodical in resolving conflicts Can connect to reality and know what is under their control and what isn't Interest in data makes them more effective listeners	Has difficulty with providing and receiving support Known to have rigid boundaries and difficulties with dealing with broader topics outside area of expertise Can struggle connecting and validating others	Work on acquiring 'human skills' and informal chitchat Get involved in wider/broader issues

SUMMARY AND ACTIONS

- The most important aspect of conflict management is the commitment to addressing the conflict and adopting the notion that this situation, as stressful as it may be, should work for you and not against you. In other words: lean into the conflict; do not avoid it.

Action plan for resolving conflicts:

- Identify the conflict and define what it is about.
- Identify the opportunity: 'If I work through this conflict, what circumstances could be improved?'

- Identify resources that could support your desired outcomes.
- Review the RESOLVE tools and decide which are the most helpful:

  ☐ Realise reality ☐ Establish clear boundaries ☐ Seek support
  ☐ Own it!

  ☐ Listen ☐ Validate ☐ Evolve
- Repeat until the conflict is resolved.

CHAPTER 7

SEVEN WAYS FOR CREATING POSITIVE CONNECTIONS

Connection gives purpose and meaning to our lives.

Brené Brown

In most martial arts, before learning to fight, one must learn the art of falling down (called Ukemi in Japanese). In this same vein, we have reviewed tools for conflict resolution before we addressed ways to create positive relationships. When you have the confidence, tools, and commitment to manage conflicts, you will be empowered and free to focus on building positive contacts. You know that if you 'fall', you have the necessary tools to get back on your feet and so does your opponent. To that end, possessing tools to resolve conflicts (RESOLVE) is an essential part of any functional and rewarding relationship. This chapter deals with creating positive connections.

Unfortunately, promoting trust and nurturing healthy workplace relationships are not a priority in many organisations, which is shocking because investing in creating supportive connections between employees can have a massive positive influence in terms of performance-related outcomes. A retired manager summarised 35 years of being actively engaged with many senior management teams in the following way, 'Unfortunately, all the teams I was part of throughout my career were pretty dysfunctional. It is sad, because of this we never got close to achieving our potential.' He is not alone. A Gallup World Poll found out that only 15% of employees worldwide are engaged in their workplaces (Clifton, 2017). Paradoxically, organisations tend to engage in organisational restricting and creating performance appraisal systems that, in many cases, end up being trust *killers. The good news is that building healthy relationships is a skill that can be learned and improved.* When you successfully improve the quality of relationships in your life, many other aspects of your daily functioning can be transformed. *It can affect everything from physical health, to overall satisfaction of life.*

This chapter will provide you with tools to:

- *create and nurture positive relationships and supportive work environments*

- *accurately assess your relationships*

- *have a reality check by receiving feedback about how others perceive your ability to relate*

- *make a plan to address your areas of weakness in relationship-building.*

Human relationships by their very nature are often both rewarding and difficult. Relationships in the workplace are especially challenging because you spend many hours at your workplace and, more often than not, you don't get to choose your co-workers. Further, the structure of most professional environments renders itself to power play dynamics, which may challenge your sense of self-worth. Also, many of your gifts and talents may stay in the shadows, unless they are needed to perform your day-to-day duties. For example, if you are an engineer, you probably won't be recognised at work on your ability to play a piano sonata, or your outstanding strategic chess skills. And, to top it off, when that inevitable argument with a supervisee or supervisor occurs, you won't have the option to go to a couple's counsellor (even though that can be an effective solution!).

One of the main myths regarding interpersonal relationships is that connection is some kind of 'chemistry' over which we have very little control. Simply stated, 'we "click" or we don't and it cannot be helped either way'. If I 'click' with my supervisor or supervisee, my work life will be that much easier than if I don't. The reality is that connection is an interaction that can be broken down to its basic ingredients. When we look at each ingredient and then at how they correspond with each other, we get a better understanding of the art of connecting. In order to help you improve your interpersonal connections, we have developed a tool to help you quantify connection, measure the strength of a specific relationship, and identify opportunities for its improvement. This tool helps to break down an abstract concept into observable behaviours.

We first identified seven aspects of healthy relationships and constructed practical tools that can create positive workplace connections. Most of them are also applicable to all interpersonal relationships. There is a famous Jewish-Hasidic story of a man who, upon his death, met with the Creator, and was faced with the option of choosing between Heaven and Hell. He was surprised to discover that both places looked pretty much the same! But, in Hell, the people could not feed themselves because the forks they were given were too long to handle and, hence, they were ravenously hungry. While, in Heaven, the forks were also absurdly long, but nobody starved, because people fed each other.

Our hope is that improving your ability to implement small steps in the way you connect will allow you to experience 'heaven' in your workplace.

SEVEN WAYS TO CREATE AND IMPROVE POSITIVE CONNECTION IN THE WORKPLACE

COMMITMENT AND LEVEL OF VALUE (LOV)

Creating and improving existing relationships is an art form that requires deliberate intention, energy and effort. You wouldn't want to waste those resources on relationships that are not truly important to you. You can use the stakeholders map in Chapter 2 to help you assess how much you are willing to invest in building a connection with a specific person. Don't be discouraged by a dysfunctional or bad relationship. This chapter is about improving those relationships to work in your favour.

Determining how valuable a relationship is

Name of the person: _____

Rate how valuable this relationship is to you (1 not important to 10 very important):

_____

Why did you give this relationship this rating? _____

_____

Are you willing to invest time to improve this relationship? _____

If the answer is no, let it go. If yes, move on to an action plan (which will be described in detail in this chapter).

TRUST

The ability to trust and be trusted is the foundation of relationships. Your trustworthiness can always be improved and deepened. Bill's story is a manifestation of the power of trust to produce amazing results.

Bill was hired to develop a new and innovative product for an established company. Doing his work required introducing new procedures and workflows for the staff of the organisation. This change was met with resistance by the employees. The path to implementing his new product was full of obstacles. Several directors tried to guide Bill, but they were unsuccessful, due to their lack of knowledge in his specialised field. They failed to understand what Bill needed and how to support him when things didn't go as well as planned. Eventually, the chief finance officer, Katrine, stepped in to take over this necessary supervisory role. Katrine was reluctant to do it because, like everybody before her, she had little insight into the new product and the procedures required to build it. So, she decided it was time for her to learn.

First, she focused on learning the product and understanding Bill's needs at the company. Very quickly, a bond of trust was created between Bill and Katrine. During this time, the product started to develop at an exponential pace. It was successful in every measurable matrix and the staff smoothly adapted to the new procedures. Bill told us, 'I was "in love" with the company and with my job. Each day we had a breakthrough and, when we faced setbacks, I didn't waste unnecessary energy worrying about it. Instead, Katrine and I focused on solutions and empowering each other. I woke up each day looking forward to the day ahead. The active ingredient in this relationship was first and foremost *trust* and the commitment to stay honest and engaged, even when it was hard. We dealt with many internal and external obstacles. Those were the most productive and fun years of my working life. Since then, I have developed many products, but I was never able to replicate this same success because since then I never had that kind of trust and support.' The big challenge with trust is that it is built slowly by many little daily acts and it can be tarnished by one unintentional act of betrayal.

The good news here is that trust can be restored. In reality, when trust is violated and then, subsequentially, fully repaired, this new trust is stronger than it was initially. Horsager (2012), an adjunct professor of organisational leadership at Bethel University, defined trust as 'the ability to believe in a person or a product as having inherent integrity, even under the most trying circumstances'. He gives examples of how greater trust translates to greater creativity, freedom, morale and productivity. He names the 'Eight Pillars of Trust': clarity, compassion, character, competency, commitment, connection, contribution and consistency.

Rebuilding broken trust

The method for rebuilding broken trust can be summed up in the four As model (AAAA):

- **Acknowledge:** what happened in detail and verify that the person you are addressing feels you 'got it'.

- **Apologise:** take full responsibility and use the sentence: 'I am sorry I did XYZ (whatever the situation was as objectively as possible), and I understand that it was annoying/disappointing/hurtful/harmful to you.' Avoid (at all costs!) adding any 'but' because it then discounts everything stated before the 'but' . . . For example: 'I apologise for doing X *but*, you did Y.' 'Butting' is never a good idea and brings in blame to the person to whom you are apologising.

- **Amend:** be active in addressing and fixing the situation. Demonstrate by actions that you understood what went wrong and you are taking steps to rectify your mistake or prevent its reccurrence in the future. Often, actions speak louder than words.

- **Agree:** and make plans to move forward.

SAFETY

Physical safety is a basic human need. When it is violated or compromised, all other aspects of any relationship are in danger. We shall continue under the assumption that your organisation prioritises physical safety.

In order to have positive relationships, we also need to have *psychological safety*. Edmondson (2019), a Harvard Business School professor, explains in her book *The Fearless Organization*, the need for psychological safety, which means that people within the organisation are protected from being ridiculed or punished for speaking up. It is a common practice in many organisations to discourage people from expressing opinions that are contrary to the ideas defined by the management team. This dynamic is usually implicit and hidden. Actually, in many organisations where 'speaking your mind' is discouraged, the explicit message is: 'we respect you and we want to hear what you have to say', but, in reality, expressing ideas that are controversial or contradict what is already in place are discouraged and people violating this unwritten rule may find themselves shamed or covertly looked down upon by management or even their co-workers.

A good example for that is John's story. He came to therapy after he wrote an email to his supervisor and her peers suggesting some ways to improve the workflow in his company. He also asked some valid questions about the current procedures in his email. He received a return email from a member of the senior management team, requesting him to be more mindful about clogging their inboxes with these 'non-urgent' questions. His email was never addressed nor were his valid points ever considered. Since then, his morale has plummeted – he has never made any additional suggestions, and gone on to poorly perform his duties as outlined in his job description. In any working relationship, knowing that you can express your thoughts, opinions, and even doubts, is a signature sign of psychological safety.

Increasing safety

Psychological safety is addressed by creating a space, where you express yourself without fear of adverse outcomes. Try the following exercise to assess how you may rank in providing a safe space at work.

Creating safety requires honesty and taking a candid internal inventory:

- Am I deeply open and interested in hearing my employees', co-workers', or supervisors' opinions and ideas?
- Are there any subtle ways in which I limit people's expressions and ideas (e.g. like being impatient, criticising them behind their backs, not taking them seriously, joking in a nonchalant way about what they are saying)?
- Am I committed to change and self-improvement?
- Do I make myself approachable and available to my colleagues and teams?

Make a plan to address the areas you can improve.

When you work in a workplace that lacks psychological safety, your options and success are limited.

You can consider the following:

- Be fully aware of your boundaries: what are you willing to do and what not? (For example, are you willing to work overtime and/or on weekends? What are the job assignments you can perform, what are the ones you can't? How do you want to be addressed? What workplace behaviours are acceptable to you and which ones are not?) Make a list, stay true to yourself while staying as flexible as practically possible, be clear about your boundaries and express them, commit to acts aligned with your values, and choose your battles wisely.
- You can write an anonymous letter to the senior management team or board of directors, with practical solutions.

- Buy someone in a position of power a book that can help him or her understand what the problem is. Highlight the relevant pages.

- Explain how you see the problem, and outline your suggestions. Be respectful to your colleagues and don't forget to mention what is going well and correctly.

- Ask relevant people if they are interested in receiving your feedback.

- If everything else fails, work on your exit plan from the organisation.

INTEGRITY

There is a common myth that, in order to succeed, you need to cheat, lie and manipulate. The reality is that lack of integrity is extremely damaging in relationships. It might present some gains in the short term, but it is a losing strategy in the long term. It might occasionally seem the easiest way out of difficult situations, but it truly isn't. There is a power in truth that lends itself to safety and loyalty in self and others. When someone knows that they can trust your word, they will be much more inclined to want to truly collaborate with you. Furthermore, when you demonstrate integrity, it encourages others to increase their level of integrity too. This is not to be confused with self-righteousness and pretending to be holier than thou. The consequences of being disloyal and deceiving are not only in the tangible outcomes that are eventually poor but in internal well-being. When someone lies and deceives others, this person must assume that others do the same. It translates to paranoia and being constantly on guard. As psychologists, we get to witness people 'back stage', the side of them they usually hide from the world. From this perspective, we can safely testify to the hellish world of living without being able to trust.

Tami learned a vital lesson in honesty early on. As a young theatre director, she was interviewed for a prestigious scholarship, for which her odds of receiving were slim to none. She told the director who interviewed her about difficulties she was facing in a production she was directing. The director seemed surprised and Tami explained: 'It is not that I am honest, I am just too tired to lie.' She received the scholarship that made a fundamental change in her professional life. The director told her later, 'It is your honesty that made us believe that you were the person we were looking for.'

Honesty is the best policy not just in the scholarship arena or in the theatrical world. Several studies showed that families and patients were less likely to sue in cases of adverse reaction to treatment when provided by medical doctors with a full explanation and apology (Hickson et al., 1992). It is not a formula or an agreement that means: 'I am going to tell you the truth and you will give me what I want.' It only means, 'I am going to play fair, because this is how I choose to show up myself to the world.'

One of our clients stated, 'I want my grandchildren to be proud of me. It means that sometimes I have to sacrifice things I want. I usually want to win but I choose to lose if it jeopardises my ability to sleep at night or my legacy.'

You can test your integrity by candidly answering the following questions:

1. Do I often lie to the people I work with?
2. Do I often gossip about others?
3. Do I often 'cut corners'?
4. Do I often pretend to know more than I actually know?
5. Do I often present myself differently before the people I supervise and my supervisors?
6. Do the people around me know what I think about them?
7. In percentage terms, how much of what I say I am going to do do I actually do? _____

The answers to these questions do not reveal how high you succeeded to climb in your organisation or company, they mainly reveal your quality of life. We all lie, gossip, cut corners, cheat and pretend from time to time. It is part of being human. We, the authors, needed to look at our integrity while writing this chapter and it wasn't easy. We suggested being aware of our shortcomings and correct the behaviours that are not aligned with our integrity, the way we want to be treated and the people we want to be.

RESPECT

Respect is a feeling of safety and trust with the addition of seeing others in their best light possible, to see them as successful, talented and capable. The Sanskrit word *Namaste* represents the concept, 'I bow to the light inside you'. It is obviously easier said than done. There are some scientific references to the effectiveness of seeing (or bowing to) a person's potential. One is the Pygmalion effect, which refers to the phenomenon that when we perceive people as capable, this will positively affect their performance. Robert Rosenthal and Lenore Jacobson (1992) showed that student performances were positively correlated to teachers' expectations. This correlation is alive and well in the workplace. If you believe in an employee's ability to perform well, chances are that he or she will. It is not a magical unexplained phenomenon. When you expect someone to do well, you tend to be more aware of things that are going well, you recognise those behaviours, and reward them, that in turn motivates the person to repeat this behaviour. Michelangelo (Parker, 2013), the famous artist, stated: 'I saw the angel in the marble and carved until I set him free.' The pre-requisite for this powerful dynamic to work is you cannot fake it, you need to see the light in others. You truly need to 'see the angel'.

It is not recommended to be naive and neglect to see areas that need to be corrected. On the contrary, seeing people as competent and able allows them to provide honest feedback which is a huge gift in the workplace. Providing respectful feedback sends the message that you trust them and want to help them be the best they can be.

EXERCISE

Respect in action

Focus on one person who you may see in an incompetent light. See everything that is positive about them. Write it down:

1.

2.

3.

Remind yourself of this list each time you interact with him/her. Repeat until you can observe noticeable changes in the way you feel about this person and/or the way this person behaves towards you and his/her work.

ABILITY TO TAKE RISKS

> *There are risks and costs to a program of action. But they are far less than the long-range risks of comfortable inaction.*

> John F. Kennedy

Connecting requires taking risks. In the workplace, there is a constant temptation to avoid risks and stay inside our comfort zone. This is completely understandable because the consequences of saying or doing the wrong things might end up in your having to look for another job. Yet, it is avoiding risks that makes us stagnate and waste precious years of our life! There is something paradoxical in escaping risks because it gives us the illusion that we are safe. This dynamic is happening in our mind. We avoid taking risks, the 'horrible' consequence we imagined does not happen so we feel safe and encouraged to continue shunning moving out of our comfort zone. Treasurer (2019), in his book *Courage Goes to Work*, explains how avoiding moving forward and taking risks can impede employees' careers. He suggests four steps in his 'Courage Foundation Model': jump first, create safety, harness fear and modulate comfort. If avoiding risks is a major issue in your life, we strongly recommend reading his book. We are not denying that taking risks is scary, but we suggest finding the courage to take the next small step towards what you want to achieve.

One risky behaviour in the workplace is giving feedback. Sincere positive feedback is a true gift. Noticing and rewarding positive behaviour naturally makes people motivated to repeat those behaviours. Negative feedback can be devastating but, equally, it can be empowering. Kim Scott (2017) explains how guidance is a key to creating a joyful team. She states that the core of effective feedback is caring personally and challenging directly. Successful organisations implement this attitude, There is no bad feedback, but there are bad situations due to lack of feedback.

EXERCISE

Take a step outside of your comfort zone

Identify a relationship you want to focus on improving:_____

What do you want to achieve? _____

What is the next appropriate step you can take in order to achieve these outcomes? _____

_____

It is equally important to seek feedback and accept it. It might feel awkward to ask for feedback, especially when there is a power dynamic in place, but it is as important as having a good map when you are navigating in the wilderness. Soliciting feedback, evaluating it, and allowing this feedback to affect you will help you arrive at your desired destination.

EXERCISE

Find an area you are interested in improving and ask for feedback from someone who knows your work in this arena.

MINDFULNESS

Mindfulness calls for paying attention, being aware and accepting what is without judgement. At work, many facets are competing for your attention. It is easy to get distracted, stressed and overwhelmed. Focusing on your own behaviour in the present, as well as noticing others, can be beneficial. This can help you change and avoid destructive patterns of behaviours. Being mindful can help you reduce stress and increase your ability to think clearly, be more engaged, and enjoy the present moment. It can also help you identify destructive patterns of thinking and behaving. Once you identify and see an obstacle, it is easier to go around it.

The way we grow and evolve by increasing awareness is well explained in Portia Nelson's (1977) poem *Autobiography in Five Short Chapters*. She describes the progress of learning to avoid obstacles as first falling into a hole, not taking any responsibility, then recognising what we did, but still falling into the same pattern (hole) until we learn to see the hole and avoid it. Eventually, we find a new path and altogether avoid the street where the hole is.

In recent years, being attentive to the present moment became a trend. There are many books, apps and programmes that help you become more focused and mindful. In terms of relationships, being mindful truly allows you to track your thinking and be more intentional in the way you act.

EXERCISE

Ways to become more mindful

1. *Set a clear intention to be present and notice when you may get distracted.*

2. *Take breath breaks. A few times a day, just stop and follow your breath for five minutes. Be aware of the notion of breathing. Notice yourself breathing in and out and how your body and mind change when you follow your breath. Focus on one task and make mental notes of what you are doing.*

3. *Pay attention. Look at someone at work and notice something about him/her you did not notice before.*

4. *Find time to meditate. There are many apps that can help you find a meditation that will work for you.*

The next exercise will give you a snapshot of any relationship that you are interested in exploring. You can complete a snapshot of this connection at different levels, including: self, others, groups, organisations and communities and concepts. It can increase your awareness of both weak and strong aspects of this relationship.

Connection snapshot: rating connections in your life

Choose a relationship with a person in your life or workplace. Rate each statement on how true this statement is: 1 not true at all and 10 absolutely true.

Start rating how important this relationship is to you: _____.

We recommend that you don't invest too much time or energy into relationships that are lower than 5.

Statement	Rating: 1 (low) to 10 (high) Add any comments
1. I can trust this person.	
2. I feel safe with/around this person. I can speak my mind.	
3. My boundaries (needs and wants) are accepted and respected.	
4. I feel respected by this person.	
5. I feel I can take risks and go outside my comfort zone with this person.	
6. This person is attentive to me. I feel seen and understood.	
7. I feel this person welcomes feedback.	
8. I appreciate this person's feedback.	
9. I can admit my mistakes easily and this person admits mistakes too.	
10. I feel I can grow and change within the frame of this relationship.	
Total score:	

If you scored:

- *85–100: Excellent! Continue doing what you are already doing.*
- *70–84: Room for improvement – look at areas for improvement. Choose one and add it to your action plan (at the end of this chapter).*

- *51–69: Need for significant change. Choose two areas of focus and add them to your action plan.*
- *40–50: Requires radical change.*
- *Less than 40: Is this relationship really important to you? Consult with someone about what you can do or accept things the way they are.*

EXERCISE

Questions for reflection

- *What are the main ingredients that impact the low/high results?*
- *Does this reflect any of your personal patterns?*
- *What's your role in this? What's in your control? In which areas can you flex/ change?*
- *What are possible first next steps?*

Another powerful exercise you might want to try is rating yourself on the following set of statements and then elicit feedback from three to five colleagues. Ask them to rate you on the same statements. Your connection rating would be the average rating that others gave you. You will discover how you are perceived by others and what they think about your ability to connect. The more people you ask to complete this short survey, the more information you will have to work with. Your connection rating constantly changes, It is context-related, it change as you work to improve it. Using these simple tools to quantify your ability to connect will help you identify which areas to focus on. You might have a high connection rating at home and a poorer one at work or vice versa.

Soliciting feedback can be risky; it puts you in a vulnerable position, but it can give you valuable information. It validates things you are doing well and also identifies areas you can improve upon. As we stated previously: *feedback is a gift*.

One way that we have found effective in asking for feedback is to say or write to people: 'I am working on improving my ability to connect. I am devoting time and effort to this process. I appreciate your opinion [only if you sincerely do] and I will be grateful if you would be willing to complete this brief five-minute survey.'

If needed, find ways to make this survey confidential. If it is not anonymous, reassure people that there would be no adverse consequences of completing the survey. In return, you might have a better boss/colleague/friend or family member from the experience.

Connection rating (CR)

Ask your target audience:

- *Please rate me on a scale of how much this statement is true about me in the frame of our relationship: 1 not true at all, through 10 absolutely true.*

Statement	1 (low) 10 (high)
1. You can trust me.	
2. You feel safe around me. You can speak your mind freely around me. You feel that I respect your boundaries (i.e. needs and wants). Now average the score on those two answers to get a score on safety.	
3. You feel respected by me.	
4. You feel that you can take risks and go outside your comfort zone in my presence.	
5. You feel that I am attentive when we interact. You feel seen and understood by me.	
6. You receive honest and effective feedback from me.	
7. I accept your influence. You feel that I appreciate your feedback and make changes accordingly.	
8. You perceive me as a person who admits mistakes.	
9. I help you grow and change.	
10. I go the extra mile for you.	
Total survey score:	

If this is not done anonymously, you could use the information in this survey to have an open conversation with the person who rated you. If you are interested in this, ask for the person's consent. Let them know you might be interested in discussing their survey results with them afterwards. Verify that this is OK with them. When you have all the information, refer to the appropriate sub-section in order to get ideas on how to improve your connection rating and create healthy relationships.

SUMMARY AND ACTIONS

Improving our relationships is an ongoing process. It requires intention and constant attention. We believe that it is one of the best investments you can make for yourself. Like many other personal changes, you cannot do this overnight. The most effective way to achieve results is by setting an intention and implementing small but consistent steps. There are things you can do on a daily, weekly, monthly, and even a yearly, basis.

Step one: define what relationship you want to improve.

Step two: assess the current situation:

1. Complete the connection rating for this person. If possible and safe, ask them to rate you (don't take unnecessary risks at this stage, however). Identify areas of strengths and areas in need of improvement.

   Rating: _____

   Areas of strengths: _____

   Areas in need of improvement: _____

2. If you are working on your own CR, identify an area you would want to improve in your connections (e.g. work, with family, or with friends) and ask people to complete the survey.

   Rating: _____

   Areas of strengths: _____

   Areas in need of improvement: _____

Step three: intention:

1. Set a clear intention. (What do you want to experience within this relationship?)

2. If you are working on your CR, define what ultimate outcome you want to see for yourself.

Step four: importance:

Rate the level of importance (value) of this relationship:

Write down why it is important: _____

Step five: define the action steps on a daily, weekly and monthly basis:

- On a daily basis: I will . . . (e.g. find something positive about this person or others, write a human gratitude list, at the end of the day write down what I am grateful for or do something nice for this person, be attentive to this person's needs).

- Once a week: I will . . . (e.g. do something special for this person, invite them out, send a supportive email, tell someone else about what I find special in this person).

- Once a month: I will . . . (e.g. elicit feedback, go out of my way to do something really special, give this person a gift just because . . .).

Step six: feedback:

At the heart of change is feedback. Let a person you trust know what you are doing, and ask him or her to give you honest feedback. Re-do the rating exercise. Modify your action plan accordingly.

Good luck and cheers to improving a vital component in your relationships!

PART III

HOW TO IMPROVE COMMUNICATION AND WORKING RELATIONSHIPS

CHAPTER 8

HOW TO CONNECT ACROSS CULTURES

Culture is to society what memory is to individuals.

Clyde Kluckhohn

Organisations are becoming much more diverse with diffused labour and rapidly expanding global cooperation and markets. Technology that allows instantaneous contact with anyone in the world results in a world in which geographical boundaries can no longer divide and insulate. It is imperative for leaders to connect with others across different national cultures. However, in order to be effective, it is vital to combine both self-awareness of your connector type (as provided in Chapters 3 and 4) with an increased awareness of the impact of national culture at work. Unless you are willing to reflect on the impact of yours and others' cultural values, these can emerge from 'beneath the surface' and surprise you when you are least expecting it. Campbell et al. (2008) argued that lack of cross-cultural understanding is a value destroyer, resulting in a loss of billions in failed mergers. If not addressed, lack of cultural awareness can significantly damage business relationships with key stakeholders, undermining team working, and ultimately the quality and timely delivery of projects.

This chapter will give you the ability to:

- *raise your awareness of national cultures and their implications at work*

- *increase your ability to lead change in a diverse environment by avoiding 'culture surprises', and improve your range of leadership behaviours to deliver effectively with others*

- *learn how to shift your mindset from a local to international leader/ manager.*

On 17 June 2000, Glaxo Wellcome and SmithKline Beecham (SKB) announced one of the biggest mergers in UK corporate history, creating the world's largest drug firm, worth $187 billion (see BBC News, 2000).

The two companies had tried to merge before but were not successful. Jan Leschly (Danish/US national), the CEO of SKB, was due to be the boss of the merged entity and Sir Richard Sykes (British national), the CEO of Glaxo Wellcome, the chair of the joint business. Due to a clash of egos/cultural backgrounds between them, the merger was aborted. The CEOs could not agree on who would run the joint company, resulting in a loss of billions to shareholders. According to Ferrell et al. (2011), Leschly had a strict management style and came from an SKB performance management culture. This contrasted with Sykes' scientific-based approach and traditional style of management. The top executives came from different cultural backgrounds which were not compatible. Sykes was modest and reserved in line with English national characteristics. Leschly was much more extrovert (a well-known tennis player) and with a personality that matches typical US characteristics (e.g. extroverted and direct). The inability to connect due to national cultural differences was a critical factor in the breakdown of relationships and the eventual failed joint merger. Only after Leschly retired in 2000 did the merger go through under the leadership of Jean-Pierre Garnier (see BBC News, 2000).

In the first part of this chapter, we outline a framework for categorising cultures and provide real life examples of how national cultures collide at work. This is followed by tips on how to communicate in the various cross-cultural set ups, in order to overcome these misunderstandings. In the second part, we offer a simple test to assess whether you are potentially a local or international manager, followed by key recommendations on how to shift from local into effective international management.

WHY SHOULD YOU BOTHER WITH NATIONAL CULTURE?

Geert Hofstede (see Hofstede et al., 2010), a key researcher in the area of national culture and its impact at work, has studied 50 countries over 40 years, and is the originator of a comprehensive framework for categorising cultures. He argued that culture is 'programming of the mind'. It is the shared mental programme of human beings that differentiates one national culture from another. National cultural norms and values are developed at an early stage and are the internal dictionary that influences how we make sense of the world.

Norms are taken for granted and can cause misunderstandings and poor communication in teams operating across geographical boundaries. They will determine whether people will prefer meetings with or without an agenda or will insist on a written contract instead of an informal handshake. National culture will also be a significant factor in people's energy for completing tasks in a timely manner, in contrast to being much more relaxed about deadlines; if talking and addressing conflict openly is encouraged or not; whether decision making is top down or by consensus.

When we embark on business outside our own national cultural borders, we start noticing cultural assumptions coming into play. These are so ingrained that they rule our behaviours automatically. The only solution for bridging between differences is to increase our understanding of the cultural context. It is our responsibility as managers/leaders to address and bridge these differences with courage and wisdom.

When dealing with culture, there is an interesting phenomenon in which behaviour predictions are accurate and inaccurate, at the same time. Hofstede used a large amount of data to provide predictions on cultural characteristics, which most of the time are accurate. Nevertheless, there are pertinent individual differences that need to be considered, including gender, position in the family of origin, life events and the social environment.

On top of national differences, there are other significant differences stemming from the various functional cultures. Engineers have their own unique style which is very different from sales/marketing. Corporates have their own distinct culture too. IBM, as a company, is very different from Apple.

FRAMEWORK FOR CATEGORISING CULTURES

Hofstede's (see Hofstede et al., 2010) framework has five key dimensions that are used to classify national cultures (see the table below).

Dimension	Power differential (PD)	Individualism (IND)	Masculinity (MAS)	Uncertainty avoidance index (UAI)	Long-term orientation (LTO)
High	Centralised Strong hierarchies Large gaps in compensation, authority, and respect	Value on people's time and need for freedom Enjoyment of challenges Expectation of rewards for hard work Respect for privacy	Men masculine, women feminine Well-defined distinction between men's work and women's work	Lots of rules and policies Need and expect structure Expression of emotions	Family = basis of society Parents and men have more authority than young people and women Strong work ethic High value on education and training
Low	Flatter organisations Supervisors and employees considered almost as equals	Emphasis on building skills Work for intrinsic rewards Harmony more important than honesty	A woman can do anything a man can do Powerful and successful women are admired and respected	Informal business attitude Long-term strategy > daily basis Accepting of change and risk	Promotion of equality High creativity, individualism Treat others as you would like to be treated Search for self actualisation

Below is a detailed explanation of how each dimension and cultures can collide at work.

The first dimension is the *power differential* (PD). This is about a degree of inequality that exists and is accepted among the people in society, with and without power. A high PD score implies that the society accepts an unequal distribution of power and people understand 'their place' in the system. In high PD countries, such as Japan, Italy and Indonesia, organisations will have centralised and strong hierarchies. There will be large gaps in compensation, authority and respect. Managers are expected to come up with answers to questions. This contrasts with cultures with low PD scores. In the Netherlands and Sweden, good managers consult with their staff. It is a sign of strength to say you don't know and staff don't respect leaders who decide it all themselves. In these cultures, members of society view themselves as equals. It is common to have flatter organisations with smaller power differences. Supervisors and employees are considered almost as equals.

In Novo Nordisk (an international pharmaceutical company with its HQ in Denmark, a low PD country), employees at all levels, including top executives, have lunch in one dining area. However, in Pfizer (a global pharmaceutical company, with its HQ in NY/USA, a medium PD culture), executives and staff do not mix during lunch. They have separate dining areas. Another case study that shows the clash between high PD and low PD cultures is the merger between Volvo and Ford.

CASE STUDY

Merger integration at Ford and Volvo

In 1999, Ford acquired Volvo. It brought together two complex organisational structures with very different cultures. The success of the merger depended on a smooth and clear decision-making process between the research and development (R&D) of the two companies. It was evident from the outset that there were differences in approach. Ford engineers (US/medium PD score) passed decisions on to top management. This contrasted with Volvo (Swedish/low PD score) who were expected to take team decisions at speed. This clash of national cultures led to constant confusion about where the decision-making responsibility lay and a longer post-merger integration process.

Top tips for operating in a high PD culture (significant gaps in power within the society):

- Be aware of the key people at the top of the organisation that need to approve key decisions and influence them without the positional power.
- Skilfully challenge the leaders at the top of the organisation by inquiring into the decision-making process and using both qualitative data (e.g. client stories) and best practice/evidence.

Try to use these phrases:

- 'Who do I need to convince the senior leadership to make this happen?'
- 'I value your views (senior executive) and would like to suggest that you look into this report.'
- 'How about we involve other people from other functions into this strategic conversation?'

Top tips for operating in a low PD culture (equal distribution of power within the society):

- Be politically aware and navigate the hierarchy sensitively so that you are accessible to people at all levels of the organisation.
- Flex your leadership style, slow down and use teamwork to involve as many people as possible in the decision-making process.
- Bring in connector types (such as innovator/director/specialist) to maximise the impact on the task.

Try to use these phrases:

- 'What do you think about this idea? I would value your input.'
- 'Can we touch base for coffee next week? I would like to informally discuss a report that I am preparing for the board.'

EXERCISE

Please reflect on the following questions:

- *Is your organisation high power or low power?*
- *How does it play out in your organisation?*
- *What are the implications for you at work?*

Try this today:

- *Talk to someone from a different national culture (either low PD or high PD).*
- *What did you learn?*

Next week, try this:

- *Think of a difficult relationship/project and the person's national culture (either low PD or high PD). Aim to use one of the above suggested phrases.*
- *What did you learn?*

The second dimension in Hofstede's framework is *individualism* (IND). High IND cultures value people's time and need for freedom. People appreciate challenges and expect rewards for hard work. In Germany, UK/USA (high IND cultures), there is respect for privacy. There is a loose connection between people and relatively little interpersonal connection at work. People are close to family and several close friends. This differs from a society with a low IND score (Singapore, Vietnam, Nigeria, China). Here, there will be an emphasis on stronger group cohesion. They will show a large amount of loyalty and respect for members of the group. The group takes more responsibility for each other's well-being. There is an emphasis on teamwork and harmony which will be seen as more important than honesty. In low IND cultures, building relationships is vital for team working and work and personal lives overlap. Social talk builds personal trust and confidence.

Dutch ex-pat in Nigeria

A Dutch executive (high IND) was relocated to Nigeria (low IND). When interacting with others, she did not share much about her private life, did not show personal interest in others and was mainly task-focused. However, she failed to realise the importance of national culture. In Nigeria, there is a vastly different norm around relationships at work. It is vital to build personal relationships with others, ask personal questions on the family/personal life, before moving into meetings/work. Because of a lack of cross-cultural awareness, she came across as aloof and uninterested, which, ultimately, impacted her ability to form good relationships with colleagues. The ex-pat derailed and her credibility within the business was damaged. The overseas assignment came to an abrupt ending.

German working etiquette (using *Sie* and *Du* in business)

When working in Germany (high IND culture), the norm is to address people in a formal way (e.g. *Sie*). Over time, when you get to know each other, you move to addressing each other using *Du* which is informal, although you need to be careful not to assume and check your personal closeness before using an inappropriate way of approaching someone. In high IND cultures, assuming personal intimacy too quickly can derail the relationship and you may appear as unprofessional and disrespectful of personal boundaries. If you want to shift the relationship from *Sie* to *Du*, you must consult with the person first. When coaching a German executive, Guy discussed a critical work incident where the executive attempted to shift the relationship with one of his colleagues from *Sie* (formal) to *Du* (informal). However, he was refused, leaving him highly confused, ashamed and unsure of how to proceed with an effective working relationship.

A high individualism (IND) dimension puts emphasis on the individual and a low IND score emphasises teamwork/collaboration.

Top tips for operating in a high IND culture (emphasis on individual):

- Ask questions and encourage expression of ideas.
- Make sure that you do not focus solely on functional areas and nurture meaningful relationships with others across the hierarchy.
- Don't ask for too much personal information.

Try to use these phrases:

- 'What do you think? How shall we proceed?'
- 'I would value very much your thoughts/ideas and experience in this area.'

Top tips for operating in a low IND culture (emphasis on teamwork):

- Learn how to disclose appropriately personal information, to build trust and engagement.
- Respect age and traditions and introduce change slowly. In relation to this, it is vital that you are not seen as the sole innovator and give credit to others for their accomplishments.
- Spend social time building relationships, to improve trust and 'buy-in' for your input.

Try to use these phrases:

- 'It's been a team effort . . . everyone did a great job.'
- 'It's terrific to have your insights and experience on this discussion.'

EXERCISE

Questions for reflection

- *In your organisation, is the emphasis on the individual or collaborative working?*
- *What's your preference at work?*
- *How does this impact you?*

Try this today:

- *Talk to someone from a different national culture (either low IND or high IND).*
- *What did you learn?*

Next week, try this:

- *Think of a difficult relationship/project with someone from a different national culture (either low IND or high IND). Aim to use one of the suggested phrases above.*
- *What did you learn?*

The third dimension is *masculinity* (MAS). It is about how much a society values traditional male and female roles. High MAS scores are found in countries where men are expected to be assertive and the main provider for the family. If women work outside the home, they have separate professions from men. There is a well-defined distinction between men's and women's work. Examples of such countries include Saudi Arabia, the Philippines, Italy and Japan.

In a low MAS society, the roles are not reversed but simply more blurred. Women and men work together equally across many professions. Men are allowed to be sensitive and women can work hard for professional success. Women can do anything a man can do. Powerful and successful women are admired and respected (e.g. Norway, Denmark).

Missing out on quiet voices

A male leader from a high MAS culture was leading an international team (with a mix of high and low MAS). During a teleconference, team members from the low MAS culture challenged him that he was ignoring the input of female members of the team. The leader was not aware of this unconscious pattern and started paying equal attention to the input of all team members.

CASE STUDY

Dutch business school operating in Saudi Arabia

As part of its global expansion, the business development unit of a Dutch (low MAS) business school, was requested to run an executive development programme in Saudi Arabia (high MAS). During the initial discussions, the Saudi client asked that the women (faculty) delivering on the programme follow the Hijab (Islam way of modesty) and wear a Hijab. Female academics at the Dutch Business School were surprised by this request and not sure what to do. It raised many questions. Which cultural norms do you follow? Your own or the client's? How do you handle the tension of short-term profits versus following your authentic cultural values?

Top tips for operating in a high MAS culture (values traditional male and female role):

- Ensure that you include female voices/input in the task and decision-making process.
- Be aware that people may expect male and female roles to be distinct.
- Challenge jobs and practices that are discriminatory.
- Avoid discussing emotions or making emotionally based decisions or arguments.
- Make sure that you have red lines around your core values that can't be compromised.

Try to use these phrases:

- 'I would like to organise a meeting with a diverse group of people across all the levels of the organisation.'
- 'What is our policy/practice for men and women in this area? Why is this the case?'
- 'It would be helpful to receive your feedback/views on our draft plan.'

Top tips for operating in a low MAS culture (male and female roles are blurred):

- Avoid 'old boys' club' mentality.
- Involve facilitator and innovator connector types that can maximise the input from both men and women.

- Treat men and women equally and include everyone in the conversation.
- Involve a director connector type for action and getting things done.

Try to use these phrases:

- 'I really appreciated your contribution to the meeting today.'
- 'I very much appreciated everyone's contribution today. Let's discuss the operational steps on how to take our ideas forward in the next meeting.'

EXERCISE

Questions for reflection

- *How do issues of gender play out in your organisation?*
- *What are your own views on this topic?*
- *How does this impact you?*

Try this today:

- *Talk to someone from a different national culture (either low MAS or high MAS).*
- *What did you learn?*

Next week, try this:

- *Think of a difficult relationship/project and the other person's national culture (either low MAS or high MAS). Aim to use one of the suggested phrases above.*
- *What did you learn?*

The fourth dimension is the *uncertainty avoidance index* (UAI). This dimension examines the degree of anxiety society members feel when they are in uncertain or unknown situations.

In high UAI-scoring nations, such as Russia, Japan and France, people try to avoid ambiguous situations whenever possible. They are governed by rules and order and seek a collective 'truth'. There are many rules and policies. You are required and expected to follow structure. The focus is much more on rules than on relationships. Rules should apply to all situations and people. Commitment comes from formal agreements, and refusal to have a written agreement is an insult and shows a lack of trust. It is expected to be objective in business activities and showing feelings in business is unprofessional. If you express feelings, you are likely to be perceived as untrustworthy. A low UAI score indicates the society enjoys novel events and values differences. There are very few rules and people are encouraged to discover their own truth. There is an informal business attitude and there is acceptance for continuous changes in strategy and risk. The focus is more on relationships than rules, with a belief that rules should be adapted to situations and people. Commitment comes from personal loyalty. To insist on having a written agreement is an insult and shows a lack of trust. It is as natural to share emotions as ideas and opinions. It is incompetent to hide one's feelings. Someone who expresses no feelings is regarded as cold, uncaring or untrustworthy.

International team and levels of comfort with ambiguity

An international team with mixed membership of both high and low UAI was working on a global project. Team members from high UAI cultures kept on asking for a clear plan, rules of engagement and a clear view on how to mitigate risks. However, the South American leader (low UAI) was reluctant to provide plans and process. Instead, her preference was to work in a much more emergent style, with more flexibility, dealing with issues as they arose, and focusing on the internal relationships. Following a cross-culture communication session, members of the team started to flex their approach to meet the needs of others from different cultural backgrounds. People and the leader from low UAI countries learned to work with agendas for meetings and to respect project plans/deadlines. Conversely, team members from high UAI countries adjusted to working in a more emergent way, opening themselves up to new information and opportunities.

An international German conglomerate acquiring businesses in China

An international German conglomerate had a business strategy to acquire businesses in China. Originating from a Germanic culture, which is high UAI, the structure of the business was highly centralised with many rules and procedures. During the negotiations with a potential Chinese business, they missed out on the importance of building relationships which is critical for collaboration in low UAI cultures. People trust leaders who pay attention to personal relationships instead of task-related activities. Over time, the German conglomerate had to ditch its ambitious acquisition strategy in China and focus on other geographies with more compatible cultures.

Showing of emotions during conflict

During a global project review meeting, there was a conflict around an important strategic decision. French team members were happy to show their emotions/frustrations, which was deeply uncomfortable for Japanese and Korean colleagues. Instead of ignoring this tension, the leader decided to educate and name the cross-cultural differences. It helped open up a conversation on which behaviours are acceptable in each culture and what can be done to maximise communication and avoid misunderstandings.

The (uncertainty avoidance index) UAI dimension examines the degree of anxiety society members feel when they are in uncertain or unknown situations.

Top tips for operating in a high UAI culture (people struggle with anxious/ambiguous situations):

- When possible, seek opportunities outside the agreed rules and procedures for emergent and innovative thinking.
- Be clear and concise and minimise emotions.
- Plan and prepare, communicate often and early, provide detailed plans and focus on the tactical aspects.

Try to use these phrases:

- 'It's important to consider possible scenarios to our strategy, so that we can respond well to unexpected events.'
- 'I feel the warmth and a great deal of belief in the team that we are going to be successful.'

Top tips for operating in a low UAI culture (people are comfortable in ambiguous contexts):

- Learn how to lean into ambiguity/flexible plans.
- Express your emotions through hand gestures and voice.
- Flex your approach and be prepared for changes in the plan. Express curiosity at different points of view.
- Do not impose rules or structure unnecessarily.

Try to use these phrases:

- 'I have included in this presentation the key figures and a detailed action plan for moving forward.'
- 'The structure of my presentation is . . .'
- 'In my view, the logical way forward is . . .'

EXERCISE

Questions for reflection

- *To what extent are people in your organisation comfortable with ambiguity or not? How does this play out?*
- *What is your preference?*
- *How does this impact you?*

Try this today:

- *Talk to someone from a different national culture (either low UAI or high UAI).*
- *What did you learn?*

Next week, try this:

- *Think of a difficult relationship/project and the other person's national culture (either low UAI or high UAI). Aim to use one of the suggested phrases above.*
- *What did you learn?*

The fifth dimension is *long-term orientation* (LTO). It is focused on how much society values long-standing traditions and values. In countries with a high LTO score, such as Germany and Japan, delivering on social obligations and avoiding 'loss of face' are considered very important. Family is the basis of society. Parents and men have more authority than young people and women. There is a strong work ethic and high value is placed on education and training. Disagreements are 'coded', or sent via third parties (see the figure below). Natural harmony should be maintained and expressing conflict makes both parties 'lose face'. Sensitivity to weak signals, such as tone/body language, is a highly valued skill.

What the British say	What do they mean
Not bad	Good, or very good
Quite good	A bit disappointing
Interesting	It seems rather boring to me
Oh, by the way . . .	I am about to get to the point
I hear what you say	I disagree and do not wish to discuss it any further
With the greatest respect . . .	I think that you are wrong (or a fool)
Perhaps we can consider other options	I do not like your ideas

Source: Hult/Ashridge Business School

People privilege both structure and planning. They continuously plan and manage time. You make precise appointments . . . and keep to them!

In low LTO countries, like the USA, Australia, Argentina and Angola, people put emphasis on the promotion of equality, high creativity, individualism and self-actualisation. You treat others as you would like to be treated. Open conflict is viewed as both healthy and helpful. Disagreements are openly expressed and suppressing conflict is a sign of weakness. Assertiveness is a valued skill. Appointments are intentions, and are easily changed. In order to adapt in these cultures, you have to go with the flow and be spontaneous.

Japanese and US printing companies

A Japanese company acquired a US printing company. During the post-merger integration (PMI), the US executives wanted to raise several controversial issues around strategy, vision, pay, structure of the new organisation and redundancies with their Japanese counterparts. They preferred an open and robust conversation on difficult issues. However, the Japanese management did not want to 'lose face' and wanted informal backstage conversations to resolve issues. Differences around showing emotions and feelings were also impacting the team. US folk were happy to share and publicly show emotions, while for the Japanese it was a taboo.

Over time, trust between executives across both countries eroded, resulting in plans not being implemented in an expedient manner.

CASE STUDY

Google in China

In 2006, Google (the world-famous internet giant) launched Google China. From 2006–9, market share rose from 16% to 31%. Google China developed a partnership with China Mobile, launching a customised smartphone. In January 2010, Google announced that Google China had experienced cyber attacks, targeting the Gmail accounts of several Chinese human rights activists. In March 2010, Google's HQ in the USA decided to redirect all search queries from Google. cn to Google.com.hk (Google Hong Kong), thereby bypassing Chinese regulators and allowing free flow of information. Google was caught between a rock and a hard place. In order to continue to build the business in China, it had to respect the values and traditions of the host/Chinese culture. On the other hand, these values contradict the US national values of freedom of information/speech.

The high long-term orientation (LTO) dimension values long-standing traditions and values versus self-actualisation.

Top tips for operating in a high LTO culture (values long-standing traditions and values):

- Avoid causing another to 'lose face' and do not hesitate to introduce necessary changes.
- Reward perseverance, loyalty and commitment.
- Show respect for traditions and be respectful of others.
- Do not display extravagance or act frivolously.

Try to use these phrases:

- 'I value your commitment and hard work on this project. It helped us achieve much more than we expected.'

- 'I appreciate that this is how you have been running the business for many years but we need to change several processes so that we can be more competitive in the market place. I am happy to discuss when we talk later in person.'

Top tips for operating in a low LTO culture (values self-actualisation):

- Ensure that conflict is both open and constructive. Make sure that it is focused on behavioural issues rather than personalities.

- Make sure there is not too much unconstructive conflict.

- Go with the flow. Do not overreact when someone is late for a meeting and/or changes their mind at the last minute.

Try to use these phrases:

- 'When you talked with X, it felt uncomfortable to me. It felt like you didn't value the other member's contribution. How did you feel about it?'

- 'I am happy to work with your agreed standards and policies.'

EXERCISE

Questions for reflection

- *To what extent are people in your organisation comfortable with conflict?*
- *What is your preference?*
- *How does this impact you?*

Try this today:

- *Talk to someone from a different national culture (either low LTO or high LTO).*
- *What did you learn?*

Next week, try this:

- *Think of a difficult relationship/project and the other person's culture (either low LTO or high LTO). Aim to use one of the suggested phrases above.*
- *What did you learn?*

Below is a link to an online tool that can be used to compare national cultures.

EXERCISE

Enter a national culture that interests you in the online link below:

- *Write down the high/low scores on each dimension. Was it helpful?*
- *What did you learn?*

(Visit www.hofstede-insights.com and search for 'Compare countries'.)

EXERCISE

Enter a country that you are either doing or about to do business with and your home/original country of origin:

- *Compare the two countries using the tool/link below. What are the potential tensions/surprises?*
- *Can you try one of the above suggestions to bridge the difference?*
- *What have you learned?*

(Visit www.hofstede-insights.com and search for 'Compare countries'.)

Here's an example:

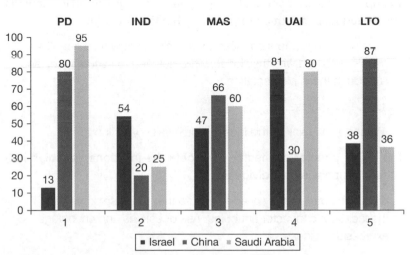

On the PD scores we notice a significant difference between Saudi/China (high PD) and Israel (low PD). This means that, in general, organisations in Saudi/China are more centralised and decisions are taken at the top of the organisation. In contrast, in Israel, there is an emphasis on equality and team working (see above for some of the tips on how you can operate more effectively in these environments). Also, you will notice significant differences in the long-term orientation (LTO) – China has a high LTO while Israel and Saudi have a low LTO. There are important implications from this piece of data. In China, you will need to be respectful of culture, traditions and how you handle conflict (e.g. avoid losing face). Nevertheless, in Israel and Saudi, the business atmosphere will be more relaxed/informal and it is assumed positive to have direct/open conflict. See further tips above.

Here are some examples of top tips for your connector type within a cross-cultural context.

Top tip for innovator connector type (makes things better) in a high PD culture (significant gaps in power within the society):

- Innovators may struggle with the hierarchical/centralised organisations and need to acknowledge the leader's power and influence them without the positional power.

Try to use this phrase:

- 'I would like to receive input from you (senior executive) on an improvement idea to help our sales process.'

Top tip for innovator connector type (makes things better) in a low PD culture (equal distribution of power within the society):

- Suitable for innovators but need to be skilful in how they get other people on board with their ideas, while needing to secure funds and support in the implementation.

Try to use this phrase:

- 'What do you think of this idea? I would value your input.'

Top tip for director connector type (gets the job done) in a high IND culture (emphasis on individual):

- Suits directors but they need to ensure that they use some of the facilitator connector attributes. Ask questions and encourage expression of ideas.

Try to use these phrases:

- 'What do you think?'
- 'How should we proceed?'
- 'I would like to hear your views.'

Top tip for director connector type (gets the job done) in a low IND culture (emphasis on teamwork):

- Directors may struggle with the emphasis on teamwork and personal relationships so need to learn how to disclose appropriate personal information, to build trust and engagement.

Try to use this phrase:

- 'I used to work in this country many years ago and experienced similar problems.'

Top tip for facilitator connector type (creates harmony) in a high MAS culture (values traditional male and female role):

- Avoid discussing emotions or making emotionally based decisions or arguments.

Try to use this phrase:

- 'I liked the logical basis for our conversation today.'

Top tip for facilitator connector type (creates harmony) in a low MAS culture (male and female roles are blurred):

- Suitable for facilitators and may need to involve other types (e.g. directors) for action and getting things done.

Try to use this phrase:

- 'It's fabulous that everyone contributed their views on this topic. Can we focus now on two to three key actions for next week?'

Top tip for specialist connector type (makes the right decision) in a high LTO culture (values long-standing traditions and values):

- Show respect for traditions and be respectful of others.

Try to use this phrase:

- 'I very much appreciate everyone's expertise and contribution to the meeting today.'

Top tip for specialist connector type (makes the right decision) in a low LTO culture (values self-actualisation):

- Go with the flow. Do not overreact when someone is late for a meeting and/or changed their mind at the last minute.

Try to use this phrase:

- 'I understand that you want me to add this piece of information at the last minute. I prefer to receive data in advance but will do my best to integrate it within the report.'

Top tip for facilitator connector in a high UAI culture:

- Instead of focusing on relationships, find out more about the country's formal rules.

Try to use this phrase:

- 'What are the expected guidelines in this area?'

Top tip for director connector in a low UAI culture:

- Where appropriate, slow down, show warmth and actively seek personal relationships.

Try to use this phrase:

- 'Please let me know how are you feeling about the progress of the project.'

ARE YOU A LOCAL OR INTERNATIONAL MANAGER?

Going through the key dimensions of Hofstede's framework will raise your awareness of both the importance and impact of national culture at work. From our experience, this will help you deal with high-stakes situations in a cross-cultural environment much more effectively. In parallel, we strongly recommend that you continue to shift your mindset from a local to an international style/perspective.

We have worked with both types of managers. The local manager is successful in relatively stable environments with homogeneous teams. His/her style is controlling which is more suitable with less skilled individuals on a straightforward task. In order to do well with this manager, you need to follow instructions, avoid conflict and/or challenging him/her. In contrast, the international manager is much more skilful, emotionally intelligent and has a facilitative leadership style. He/she will be successful in delivering on complex projects in a changing environment. They will be able to provide a psychologically safe environment for the team, where people feel empowered and able to make mistakes. At the same time, they will encourage debate, constructive debate (including challenges to their own opinions) and diversity of views. See the table below which highlights the difference between these types of managers.

EXERCISE

Assess your skills set against the table below (put a tick):

- *If needed, ask others how they view your style. If you scored fewer than five ticks, see our top tips below on how to shift from being a local to an international manager.*

You can also use this exercise within your own team:

- *As a group, do we have a local or international mindset?*
- *What are your strengths/development areas?*

Criteria	Local manger	International cross-culture manager
Control: facilitate (gives space)		
Conflict-averse: open transparent		
Lack of trust: engenders trust		
Transactional vis à vis personable/ relational style		
Low EQ vis à vis high EQ: 'can read the room'		
Focused on one approach for doing things: open/curious and Interested in multiple ways of getting things done		
Listens vis à vis talks		
Low humility/high humility		
Interested in blame: open to learning		
Needs a great deal of planning structure: comfortable with ambiguity and emergent setting		

RECOMMENDATIONS FOR BECOMING AN INTERNATIONAL MANAGER

Below are several suggestions that can help you get started. We have provided a list of actions that you can start doing today and/or next week/ month.

Today, try this:

1. **Start slow in order to go fast.**

   Cross-cultural teams have to deal with different national cultures (see earlier section), operating in different time zones with people who have varying degrees of language acumen. In our experience, it is critical to start slow in order to go fast. In practice, this means having a kick-off meeting to establish the common ground of working together, including: what's the overall task of the team? Who is doing what and what is my role? What are the 'open' as well as the 'hidden' expectations of each other? What is within our authority/control and what is not? (See more information on this in Chapter 6.) For example, what is the accepted dress code and attitude to punctuality? What is the common mode of communication (email/Skype)? When and how often do we meet face to face? How do we make decisions and resolve conflict? See other useful questions in point nine.

2. **Listen to the music behind the words.**

   Every conversation is within a cultural context which you need to tune into and understand. Under the surface of every interaction, there is an emotional reality that includes fears, intentions and feelings such as competition and envy. You can't easily tap into this information unless you are listening well (see information in Chapter 6), paying attention to body language and feelings that are part of the conversation. Some people refer to this skill as 'reading the room', understanding who the dominant person in the room is and who is not being heard. As we explained earlier, in some cross-cultural environments, especially low long-term orientation/highly coded cultures, it is vital to listen to the cues/'music' behind what's being said 'on the surface'.

3. **Insist on face-to-face connection.**

   Cross-cultural teams rely on email communications. These can be interpreted in different ways. The use of capital letters can be seen as too strong in some cultures. Not starting with 'Dear . . .' and/or stating the facts can be viewed as rude. Not adding sorry or thank you can be seen as over-aggressive when translated over different cultures. It's critical for teams to regularly meet and discuss progress, raise communication misunderstandings, and how they are doing in relation to the task. Relying solely on emails is very dangerous and can open up unnecessary conflict. A good preventive habit is to connect to discuss both the task and relationships (see further information in the next point on team maintenance).

4. **Introduce process reviews on team's maintenance.**

   Reddy (1994) (see the diagram below) argued that high-performance teams spend 70% on the task, 15% on procedures (minutes, decision-making levels, agendas) and 15% on maintenance. Maintenance means paying attention to relationships, to who is loud and who is silent, to unexpressed emotions, to the elephant in the room (if there is one!).

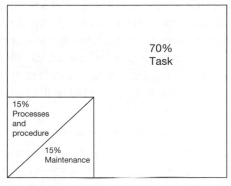

Source: Brendan Reddy, *Intervention Skills*

Some questions that you may consider for maintenance:

- What is really going on now? Are there clues that something may be going on (other than the superficial discussion, of course)?
- Is everyone agreed on the goal?
- Is the group heading in that direction? Aimlessly or over-controlled?
- What is the tone of the discussion – abstract and intellectual or emotional?
- Is the energy high or low? Rising or falling?
- What about physical posture – closed or open?
- What tension is there in the room?
- Is the discussion building on points made, or does each contribution take it off in a different direction?
- Is there a lack or excess of humour?

And other good questions:

- Are we surfacing the big issues? And approaching them directly rather than obliquely?
- Are we challenging in a helpful way?
- Are we being edgy enough?
- How are people feeling in this discussion?
- Are we recognising and tackling the elephant in the room? What might it be?

(List is adapted from a slide by Brian Marshall.)

Next week, try to do this:

5. Enhance individual's strengths.

Diversity is key to any successful team. Enhance the diversity of the team by asking individuals to undertake tasks that correlate with their national characteristics. Germans/Swedish may be better in planning. Some of your Italians and South Americans may be better in forming relationships with others. Seek to strengthen natural skills and abilities rather than amplifying individual and team weaknesses.

6. Be sensitive to space/personal boundaries.

In diverse teams, there will be different levels of expectations in relation to how much private and work life overlap. In China, you will be expected to be more open about your personal/private life than in Germany, where it will be considered rude to ask personal questions. There will be various levels of comfort with closeness/ physical space. European men/women will require more space than people in the Far East. In some Arab cultures, shaking a woman's hand is inappropriate. Tolerance to smell and body odour will differ too. Effective leaders operating in cross-cultural environments need to adapt and be sensitive to the above differences.

Over the next month, try this:

7. Build trust.

Zak, a neuroscientist and researcher, argued in a powerful *Harvard Business Review* article (2017) that, when people generate trust with each other, the brain sends chemicals (e.g. oxytocin) which make people feel more empathy towards each other and encourages taking risks and innovation. Zak argued that trust is the most powerful ingredient in any high-performing international team.

Team members in cross-cultural teams may struggle to trust each other because of some 'stereotypes' and lack of physical contact. As a leader, your role is to improve trust. Give time for people to meet each other as human beings, not just professionals 'operating behind a mask'. Trust is the fuel that will help maintain team performance.

8. **Develop your emotional intelligence.**

   Emotional intelligence (EI) is a concept developed by Goleman (1996). He argued that leaders need to have several key relational skills in order to get the most from others. These include the ability to display empathy/listening, tolerate ambiguity, communicate respect, show emotions appropriately and be flexible.

   In our experience, having EI is becoming much more significant when you are dealing with people operating with different mindsets and habits. Being open, curious and supportive to the different styles/approaches is very important. The international environment has a great deal of ambiguity. Being able to handle changes and adapt plans is critical too.

9. **Be humble.**

   Cable (2018) argued that one of the key leadership skills in motivating staff in ever changing environments is humility. Instead of the old-fashioned command and control type of approach, he suggests that leaders will ask their staff more frequently, 'How can I help you deliver excellent service?' Jungkiu Choi moved from Singapore to China to start a new role as the head of consumer banking at Standard Chartered. One of the cultural expectations was for him to visit the branches and intensify the pressures from head office to reduce costs. Instead of the formal visits, he started the day by serving breakfast to branch employees. He replaced the normal one-way PowerPoint presentations with group 'huddles', to understand from staff how he could help them improve both the performance and communication. His focus was using his power as a leader to influence rather than dictate his views. Think about how you can encourage ideas instead of compliance and fear. Jungkiu's efforts paid off. Performance, employee morale and levels of delivery have all significantly improved.

10. **Connect to others who are different from you.**

    Laura Liswood, in her book *The Loudest Duck* (2011), identified some of these 'unconscious biases' in the world of work. She argued that dominant groups in organisations (mainly white and middle class) are highly privileged and unaware of the entitlements that they receive. A white male leader in a US company will not understand the lived reality of a Pakistani (non-dominant) person within the same business. The US executive will assume that the organisation runs as a meritocracy, and will be unaware of some of the 'unconscious biases'. She raised several good questions: why do so few women run companies around the world? Why are fewer US companies run by Japanese men? Why are there more tall male leaders than short male leaders?

Fuchs, Reitz and Higgins in a 2018 *Harvard Business Review* article, built on Liswood's work. They argue that many senior leaders have an 'advantage blindness'. They are not aware of some of the automatic privileges that are part of their gender, background and role. They described an executive who was busy giving other people his opinion with very little listening to others. Being senior/white/ middle class meant that others were worried about challenging him, to the detriment of the business. Following a 360° process, the executive began to understand the importance of listening/ empathising and connecting with others who are different from him. He said, 'It's sometimes uncomfortable to just listen but that really helps me to understand what it's like for people who are different from me.'

SUMMARY AND ACTIONS

- National culture is collective programming of the mind. It is an important factor in organisational life and impacts on the extent that we are connected and our level of performance.

- When you start working with people outside your local country, you need to take into account the impact of national culture at work. Failing to do this can result in loss of personal/team effectiveness and the overall value of an acquired business.

- In order to avoid cultural surprises, it is important to open up an honest conversation on cross-national differences and implications at work.

Action plan to have a team conversation on cross-culture communication:

- Within your immediate team, reflect on the national culture of each team member.
- What are the implications for individual style/approach to work (e.g. decision making, conflict, dress code, time keeping)?
- What's your preferred style of working and how can we get the most out of your input? What are your 'red lines'?
- What are you learning as an individual/team?

CHAPTER 9

HOW TO CONNECT ACROSS AGES

The first half of our lives is usually ruined by our parents, the second half by our children.

Clarence Darrow

We start the chapter by examining some of the key changes in the digital world of work and describing each of the generations in today's workforce in more detail. We then focus on the different values and expectations between generations, especially between new recruits/ graduates (typically Generation Y) and their bosses (typically Generation X), with tips on how to turn any obstacles into opportunities. Later, we provide prompts on how to have an honest inter-generational conversation at work. This is followed by actual examples of when different generations collide at work, and further tips on how to improve both connection and communication. Throughout this chapter, we will offer exercises, checklists and recommendations on how to improve honest dialogue across the ages.

This chapter will give you the ability to:

- raise your awareness to the tensions and misunderstandings emerging from the different values and expectations of the various generations at work

- learn how to have honest conversations across generations

- leverage each generation's skills set, and utilise differences, in order to get the most from people of diverse age groups

- learn and practise new tools and actions, to increase effective communication and performance in a multi-generational team context.

It is important to bear in mind that generations are not homogenous groups. Just like any group of people, each generation is made up of individuals with differing characteristics, priorities, ambitions, circumstances and values. Therefore, it is difficult to clearly map how the various connectors relate to different age groups. Nevertheless, applying a generational lens can be a useful tool to provide a deeper insight into colleagues from different generations. Also, please be mindful that we do not always get things right first time and therefore learning from our experiences and feedback on our impact on others are vital.

WHY IS IT CRITICAL AND HOW CAN THIS CHAPTER HELP YOU?

The world of work is changing rapidly. Significant advancements in healthcare mean that people are living longer. Alongside this, government pension changes, recessions and increased living costs are also contributing to many people staying in work longer than planned. There is much talk of a four-generation or five-generation workforce, with four or five generations working alongside each other. As working until one's eighth decade becomes the norm, organisations will have an increasingly generationally diverse workforce.

Automation and artificial intelligence (AI) are transforming the workplace too. We are already witnessing automation in all businesses, with concern about the future availability of jobs being expressed across all generations. Associated with these changes, the concept of a 'career' is shifting too. The idea of a 'job for life', and the psychological contract of long-term employment with one employer over several decades, has disappeared. It is becoming increasingly common for employees to have many job roles and even several different careers during their working lifetime.

All of these changes – the diversity of the workforce, the changing work context, technological advances – raise a new set of challenges at work, highlighting the importance of understanding each generation and how they can work together in order to get the best out of an age diverse workforce.

When running a workshop with the board of a gas and oil company, Guy noticed the generational differences showing up at work. The main concern of the executives was how to fill several key vacancies for junior engineers in one of their locations in Africa. The human resource director said that she contacted several younger employees within the company's talent pool and was unable to fill the posts. Contrary to the expectations of the executives (mainly older employees), the potential candidates (younger employees) were reluctant to accept the new roles, raising issues that challenged the board, like how the relocation would impact further personal career advancement, what quality of feedback/coaching they would receive from line managers, if the company could organise a job for their partner and what the work and life balance would look like.

The senior team was highly surprised and highly annoyed. When they began their careers, employees were expected to demonstrate loyalty to both their boss and company, and to relocate in line with the company's changing strategy and needs even when this was not convenient. It was career limiting to refuse such a request from senior management. However, today's younger employees challenge some of these assumptions. This means that we need both leaders and staff across the different generations to have courageous conversations on generational differences and to explore creative ways they can work together to achieve mutually agreed goals.

INTRODUCING THE WORKFORCE GENERATIONS

There are many different definitions of birth years to categorise individuals to generations. This chapter uses the generational definitions provided in the table below. Based on these definitions, the chapter focuses on those generations that currently make up today's workforce: Baby Boomers (born 1946–61); Generation X (Gen X, born 1962–81); and Generation Y (Gen Y, also known as Millennials, born 1982–2001). It is worth noting that Gen Y's successors, Generation Z (Gen Z, born 2002–22), are quickly approaching employee age and will soon be entering the workforce too. These are the first true generation of 'digital natives' and we will soon need to consider how exactly these individuals will disrupt the workforce, and what qualities they will bring.

Over recent years, Baby Boomers, Gen X and Gen Y have made up approximately one-third of the workforce each (ONS, 2015). Previously, Baby Boomers made up the majority of the workforce, whereas Gen Y are now dominant, and will be for some time (see diagram below). Although the participation rate of Baby Boomers in the workforce has been rising, and most likely will continue to rise as people work longer, the overall percentage of Baby Boomers in the workforce is decreasing. Predictions for the next few years suggest that the workforce will be dominated by Gen X and Gen Y (Cotton, 2019; ONS, 2018).

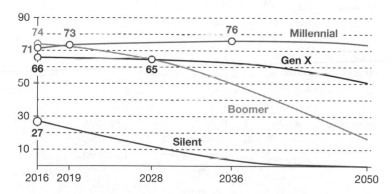

Projected population by generation (in millions)
Note: Millennials refer to the population ages 20 to 35 as of 2016.
Source: Pew Research Center tabulations of US Census Bureau population projections released December 2014 and 2016 population estimates.

Main generations in today's workforce summarised

	Baby Boomer	Gen X	Gen Y
Born	1946–61	1962–81	1982–2001
Age (years, in 2019)	58–73	38–57	18–37
Formative years/ upbringing	Post-war prosperity; booming birth rate; human rights movement; inflation; suburbia	Prosperity; globalisation; technology boom; two-earner household; corporate scandals; demand for educational achievement; MTV; AIDS; divorce	Prosperity; outsourcing; higher costs; strong political leadership; expansion of technology; natural disasters; terrorism; drugs and gangs
Key world events that changed them	Vietnam War; civil rights movement; Cold War	Assassinations of John F. Kennedy and Dr Martin Luther King; Moon landing; Death of Diana, Princess of Wales; fall of Berlin Wall; end of Apartheid in South Africa	9/11 and subsequent global wars; rapid technological change; recession
Technology	Raised with television	Technologically savvy but digital immigrants	Technologically savvy; digital natives
Learning methods	Lectures; books; courses; classrooms	Hands-on; fun; role play; PowerPoint	Mobile; Web 2.0
Relationships	**Parents:** Raised liberally **Authority:** Respect and happy to challenge status quo	**Parents:** 'Latchkey' kids; rebelled against parents **Authority:** Disinterest	**Parents:** Attention lavished on children ('helicopter' parents); opportunities provided that parents had not enjoyed **Authority:** Love/hate; suspicious; question; treat everyone as peers

	Baby Boomer	Gen X	Gen Y
Work culture	Committed; 'loyal' **Career progression:** Competitive; time served; long hours **Value:** Status and job titles **Leadership by:** Consensus	'Balanced'; 'get things done' **Career progression:** Profession rather than employer **Value:** Learning; informality; freedom **Leadership by:** Competition	'Decisive; individualistic' **Career progression:** Profession not organisation **Value:** Work–life balance; guidance **Leadership by:** Collectivism
Stereo-typical behaviours and charac-teristics	Outspoken; engaged; loyal; materialistic; powerful; passionate; idealistic; hardworking; opportunistic; powerful managers and leaders	Idealistic; individualistic; independent sceptic; self-reliant; calculating; over-reliance on technology; flexible	Confident; demanding; ambitious; optimistic; poor people skills; technologically savvy; cynical; risk averse; lack of self-awareness
Famous examples	Bill Clinton; Oprah Winfrey; Bill Gates	Michael Jordan; Michael Dell	LeAnn Rimes; Macaulay Culkin; Chelsea Clinton

EXERCISE

Can you have a conversation with someone from a different generation from yourselves on two or three dimensions using the table above? What are the similarities and differences? What may be the implications for how you view and approach work?

1.

2.

3.

GENERATIONAL GAPS – OPPORTUNITY OR OBSTACLE?

As described, employers and employees are increasingly required to manage teams comprised of members in their seventh and even eighth decade alongside those in their second. This creates a challenge for managers, leaders, organisations and HR, as well as for individuals. This can be viewed as either an opportunity or an obstacle.

In research spanning 10 years, Paine Schofield and Honoré (e.g. Honoré & Paine Schofield, 2012; Honoré et al., 2017; Paine Schofield & Franze, 2011; Paine Schofield & Honoré, 2015) have conducted studies into the global multigenerational workforce. They have gathered over 10,000 responses and conducted interviews with over 550 individuals, across all workplace generations from Gen Y to Baby Boomers. In their work, Paine Schofield and Honoré use a generational lens to explore the distinct age groups and identified gaps in how the various generational groups perceive each other. Results also show that generations differ in terms of values, priorities and expectations of work. Much of the disconnect between generations comes from miscommunication and misunderstanding. Paine Schofield and Honoré suggest that, by enabling conversations around the differences (and similarities) between generations, we can harness the benefits of a multigenerational workforce.

In the face of every obstacle lies opportunity. When people from all generations take responsibility to discuss differences across generational gaps, educate and listen to each other, communication and performance can significantly improve. The challenge is to look past the stereotypes and listen to one another. Leaders have an important role to play in this. They are required to provide a safe working environment for employees across the generations, to openly discuss differences in values, motivations and expectations. More importantly, there is a need to explore creative ways of improving communication, sharing valuable learning and experiences. Ultimately, there is a need to modify behaviours in order to accommodate people from other generations. The following table shows some of the tensions between generations and what each generation can do, to connect across the generation gap. We integrated several quotes to help clarify the expectations and priorities of each generation.

Typical generational differences for Gen X and Gen Y in work, and how to bridge them

Loyalty to employer		
Gen X expectations	Gen Y expectations	What can each generation do
Loyal to one employer 'My organisation . . .'	Less loyal to employer and much more focused on profession; seem to change employment frequently; want to be loyal but organisation needs to provide opportunities 'My profession . . .'	Gen X – be flexible and attentive to Gen Y's expectations/norm; offer coaching/great work environments/virtual comms Gen Y – adjust expectations for quick move; show commitment for the success of the business
Work and life balance		
Gen X expectations	Gen Y expectations	What can each generation do
Work hard Present in office, stay late when needed 'Work is not done and I am OK to stay late . . .'	Work–life balance; flexible working 'Can't stay late tonight as I am meeting up with my friends'	Gen X – offer great fun/environment with transparency and feedback Gen Y – offer to stay and help in critical times; be flexible about hours at work

▶

Career expectations		
Gen X expectations	**Gen Y expectations**	**What can each generation do**
Gradual career advancement based on excellent performance and hard work *'I have been working at this level for several months and need at least another year to continue to acquire new skills'*	Quick career advancement (not necessarily based on performance) *'I have been working here three months, and no one has asked me about my next job/career advancement'*	Gen X – need to be clearer on career path and what to achieve in order to progress to the next level; aim to balance both support and challenge Gen Y – need to be more patient about career advancement
Authority		
Gen X expectations	**Gen Y expectations**	**What can each generation do**
Worried about speaking up to authority and waiting for retirement *'Better not ask this question of management as I may be perceived as too difficult/ challenging'*	Happy to rock the boat and ask questions *'I want to learn and am happy to ask everything'*	Gen X – instead of being over-pleasing to 'the authorities', learn to challenge authority Gen Y – learn how to become politically savvy and when/ how to challenge superiors

Work experience		
Gen X expectations	**Gen Y expectations**	**What can each generation do**
Work experience is everything *'Our biggest issue is that Gen Y-ers/graduates do not have work experience'*	No need for work experience *'I am less interested in work experience and can learn everything from Google/the internet'*	Gen X – open up new opportunities for Gen Y Gen Y – get as much work experience; respect experience of Gen X; try as many things as possible and show willingness to learn new skills

Independent vis à vis coaching		
Gen X expectations	**Gen Y expectations**	**What can each generation do**
Independent, want to be managed autonomously (and left to get on with things) *'I am OK . . .'*	Want to be coached, and see everyone as a peer *'I am keen on your feedback/coaching'*	Gen X – develop coaching skills and allow time for feedback conversations Gen Y – seek feedback from Gen X and modify expectations for coaching

Trust and respect		
Gen X expectations	**Gen Y expectations**	**What can each generation do**
Earn respect and trust *'I am highly experienced and you (Gen Y) need to show me that I can trust you'*	Assume respect and trust *'We are all peers and can be immediately trusted and respected'*	Gen X – listen more, give Gen Y more respect and trust their actions Gen Y – understand the need to work harder in order to gain Gen X's respect

▶

Fit with organisational culture		
Gen X expectations	**Gen Y expectations**	**What can each generation do**
Expect Gen Y to fit into the organisational culture *'Our key objective is to work and achieve goals'*	Expect coaching and development *'I am entitled to feedback, coaching and development'*	Gen X – meet Gen Y's expectations and allow time for informal connections; offer coaching Gen Y – modify expectations for coaching; learn on the job, ask questions, and be independent

Communicating in a digital age		
Gen X expectations	**Gen Y expectations**	**What can each generation do**
Need to adapt to the digital revolution *'I need to improve/adapt to technology'*	Need to develop emotional intelligence and interpersonal skills *'I need to learn how to create more meaningful relationships'*	Gen X – improve digital skills Gen Y – improve social interpersonal skills; to focus on relational skills and seek feedback

Attitude to conflict		
Gen X expectations	**Gen Y expectations**	**What can each generation do**
Can handle difficult conversations *'I prefer to hear difficult/ challenging feedback directly'*	Find it difficult to have face-to-face difficult conversations *'I am pretty good and there is no need for difficult conversations'*	Gen X – focus on positives and concrete feedback, to make sure that it does not become too harsh/negative Gen Y – learn how to receive critical feedback

Relationships		
Gen X expectations	**Gen Y expectations**	**What can each generation do**
Value and invest in deep/few relationships *'Can we have coffee?'*	Good meeting strangers and OK with many superficial relationships *'Just sent a message on Twitter/WhatsApp group'*	Gen X – try to form more meaningful relationships Gen Y – to explain to Gen X benefits and learning from connecting with many people and adapt to learn how to connect in person

Learning		
Gen X expectations	**Gen Y expectations**	**What can each generation do**
You need to read/look for info *'Is there a book that I can read on this topic?'*	Everything is on Google/the internet *'Let me google it . . .'*	Gen X – learn how to access information quickly and efficiently Gen Y – try other methods/ways of acquiring information (articles/books)

Decision making		
Gen X expectations	**Gen Y expectations**	**What can each generation do**
No need to include everyone in decision making *'I am experienced and know how to lead the strategic direction of this company and who to hire'*	Need to be more transparent and open about decision making; collaborative decision making *'I would like to get involved and understand more about how we make decisions around here'*	Gen X – include Gen Y in decision making Gen Y – modify expectations and understand that Gen X-ers do not mean to exclude them from decision making; find skilful ways to get involved in the decision-making process

---

EXERCISE

Reflect on your relationship with someone you are working with who is from another generation. Can you identify two to three key differences/obstacles?

1.

2.

3.

Using the above table, what new behaviours/actions could you try to improve inter-generational communication?

1.

2.

3.

ARE YOU READY TO HAVE A ROBUST INTER-GENERATIONAL CONVERSATION?

There are similarities across generations; overall generations may be more alike than different. All generations want income, challenging and interesting work, a good work–life balance, to have a purpose and a feeling of being valued and validated. They might want these in slightly different ways. It is important to be aware of where the differences are in order to avoid negative consequences in work from stereotypes and lack of communication. It is highly important to have a conversation on these differences, whether you are a Gen Y managing Gen X-ers or the other way around. Below are several helpful conversational prompts.

Things that Gen X can say to Gen Y/Millennials:

- 'I appreciate that you prefer email communication and it would really help me if we can touch base face to face from time to time, to review my performance.'

- 'Does the level of work that you are currently undertaking match your expectations?'

- 'I value your leadership on the project. Your input was both timely and helpful.'

- 'How can we improve personal coaching and mentoring?'

- 'I have a TED talk that may be of interest to you.'
- 'I am happy for you to leave early today, but please note that we normally expect you to be at work between . . . and . . .'

Things that Gen Y can say to Gen X:

- 'If you want, I am happy to meet face to face to discuss your performance in the project.'
- 'I value your experience in this area. It's extremely valuable and can you tell/give me more information?'
- 'After completing this project, would it be OK if we give each other some feedback on both strengths and development needs?'
- 'Which of my behaviours would you like to see me do more of/less of?'
- 'It would be terrific to understand better the decision-making process in the business. I am more than happy to provide input.'
- 'How can I support you to do your work better?'

EXERCISE

Engage someone from another generation in a conversation using the prompt below:

- *'Can we talk about the differences about our upbringing and how it's shaping my behaviours today?'*

Gen X can give an example of growing up in a period without the internet and, as a result, their interest in face-to-face communication. Gen Y can share the impact of growing up during a time of rapid changes in communication and technology and, hence, the need to be connected 24/7.

- *What went well?*
- *What did you learn?*

EXERCISE

Next week, try reverse mentoring (listen to someone from another generation):

- *How do they see work?*
- *What are their values and expectations?*

Here are several helpful conversational prompts:

- *'Is the work environment conducive for you?'*
- *'How would you describe your colleagues from another generation? How would they describe you? What does this mean for effective working across generations?'*

TYPICAL EXAMPLES OF HOW DIFFERENT GENERATIONS COLLIDE AND WHAT YOU CAN DO TO BRIDGE DIFFERENCES

Now you have a deeper understanding of each generation, we will focus on how to connect effectively with each generation by providing examples of typical clashes in communication between the ages, and further tips on how to get the most out of each age group.

TYPICAL EXAMPLES OF CLASHES WITH BABY BOOMERS

During a massive organisational restructure, the board of a UK public sector organisation noticed differences in the way different age groups reacted to the proposed changes. Although Baby Boomers (commonly referred to as 'Boomers') were loyal to the company, they were resistant to change for a variety of reasons. Several managers were waiting for their retirement and were not interested in engaging with the proposed changes. Others were concerned that some of their close colleagues might become redundant. As the organisational change involved changes in the use of technology, several Boomers were extremely worried about whether they would be able to adapt. In contrast, Gen Y-ers were happy to engage with the suggested changes. In order to ensure smooth sustained organisational change, the board put more focus on communicating with Boomers about the reasons and rationale for change, responded to rumours about the loss of jobs and offered training with the new technology. Leaders initiated conversations with Boomers on the best way to utilise their energy and experience. Below is a checklist with key ideas for working effectively with Boomers.

In a family business, the founder (Boomer) of a family insisted on making the key strategic and hiring decisions on his own. His son (Gen Y) joined the company as one of the executives and demanded more transparency and involvement in the decision-making process. This clash led to growing frustration between the founder and son, who decided to seek external consultancy help. Through the conversations with the consultant, they realised that both of them needed to change. The founder needed to let go of control and lead in a much more transparent and facilitative manner. Also, he needed to trust and involve his son in the decision-making process. On the other hand, the son realised that he needed to modify his behaviours and especially learn to listen to his father's views. They may agree to differ but can still express their differences on key issues across generational divides, without falling out with each other.

HOW TO GET ON WITH BOOMERS

Here are some conversation prompts you can use when interacting with Boomers:

- 'I understand that you have been involved in this project before. Can you please share your experience? I would like to learn more from you.'
- 'I would like you to help in this area. I hear your view but let's hear from X who has new ideas that can be highly valuable for achieving your project.'
- 'I have an idea that can support your project goals, and would like feedback based on your experience.'

CHECKLIST FOR CONNECTING WITH BOOMERS

- Focus on their agenda/to do list.
- Listen to their ideas.
- Show respect for their knowledge/experience.
- Skilfully challenge their assumptions.
- Do not expect to be involved in the decision-making process.
- Be prepared to do some of the ground work/preparation before meetings.
- Be proactive in seeking personal feedback on performance.

TYPICAL CLASHES WITH GEN X-ERS

A leader (Gen X) is leading a cross-generational team. She is encountering several difficulties. Boomers prefer face-to-face meetings and find it difficult to meet using a virtual platform. Gen Y-ers want to connect online and complain about the long face-to-face meetings. In addition, the team is fragmented and there is a 'turf war' around who gets a hold of which clients. There is a great deal of unexpressed anger and conflict on how people are rewarded. Gen X-ers want to have a robust/difficult conversation on the key issues, impacting progress while Gen Y-ers want to avoid high emotions and conflict. They seem conflict-averse and find it difficult to handle criticism/negative feedback.

The leader started by having an open conversation on generational gaps and possible ways to overcome the existing difficulties. She organised face-to-face meetings with Gen X-ers, to discuss difficult issues. Similar conversations took place with Gen Y-ers via Zoom/Skype. Over time, the group started to show more respect for each other and agreed ground rules that took generational differences into account. For example, update meetings are done virtually in combination with face-to-face sessions in order to connect with each other, discuss wider strategic issues and joint working. The team agreed that it is OK to express difficult emotions and critique each other's performance.

HOW TO GET ON WITH GEN X

Here are some conversation prompts:

- 'I value your hard work and collaboration. Would you be OK to help with the report?'
- 'When possible, instead of emails, can we have face to face meetings or coffee?'
- 'I would like us to get to know each other and work on this together.'
- 'I have already done a great deal of the ground work and would value your input . . .'

CHECKLIST FOR WORKING WITH GEN X

- Explain what you need from them.
- Be independent – do not seek too much feedback/make sure that you are not over-demanding on their time/attention.
- Show respect for their loyalty.
- Ensure that there is time for face-to-face meeting.
- Develop personal relationships.
- Use their skills.
- Provide realistic plans.

TYPICAL CLASH WITH GEN Y

During a busy period in a global bank, one of the executives (Boomer) asked several Gen Y/Millennials (direct reports) to stay late and help with some unexpected work. She (boss) was surprised that they refused to help, saying that they needed to go to the gym and had made other arrangements with friends. She was not sure what to do and felt confused. These behaviours contradicted her values and expectations as a Boomer from others (see the two previous tables). After consulting with colleagues across all generations, she decided to start investing in areas that were attractive to Gen Y-ers, including: on-the-job feedback/coaching, exciting development opportunities, investment in the physical office environment, creating more fun (Boomers invited Gen Y-ers for a meal), facilitating honest cross-generational conversations about differences and expectations at work. Both performance and engagement across all ages significantly improved. In particular, Gen Y-ers were willing to go the extra mile and provide support during busy times above and beyond their formally agreed roles and responsibilities.

HOW TO GET ON WITH GEN Y/MILLENNIALS

Here are some conversation prompts:

- 'Shall we have a quick catch up afterwards to discuss how the meeting went?'
- 'I have some thoughts on this topic and here is a link to an interesting relevant TED talk.'
- 'I will need the report next week. Is this timeline OK for you?'
- 'After the meeting, I am more than happy to sit down and give you personal feedback on your performance.'
- 'Can you please send me some thoughts via email. Please let me know if I can help.'
- 'I have an idea . . . shall we set up a WhatsApp group with a few others and share some of our initial thoughts?'

CHECKLIST FOR CONNECTING WITH GEN Y

- Use technology to connect (e.g. emails/WhatsApp).
- Make them feel trusted and valued.
- Provide them with new ideas that can be implemented quickly.
- Give high personal support – coaching/mentoring.

- Provide interesting/challenging/varied work, low routine.
- Introduce rapid career progression and good work–life balance.
- Be flexible in when/where they work.
- Give public recognition for achievement.
- Ensure a good salary.

EXERCISE

Try to influence a colleague in your immediate network from another generation using one of the above optional prompts.

- *What was the impact? What did you learn?*
- *Try to resolve a generational misunderstanding using the above checklists.*
- *What surprised you? What did you learn?*

Tips for bridging generational differences
Today, try to:

- **reinterpret the intent of a comment or action** *that has annoyed or upset you and understand it differently.*

Next week, try to:

- **modify your behaviour to be more in sync with the other person** *to facilitate improved communication. Ask them 'What do you need from me?'*
- **link Boomers and younger generations in mixed teams** *for mutual benefit – find creative ways of achieving goals with mixed groups.*
- **increase trust.** *Demonstrate that you care about Gen Y-ers. Embed feedback in performance management and invest in the physical environment. Find opportunities to have fun together over a social activity/ lunch. Share personal (even embarrassing) stories.*

Next month, try to:

- **challenge leaders to go beyond the rhetoric.** *Stimulate and amplify behaviours that represent the desired culture. Align leaders' behaviours (in particular coaching).*

- **set expectations with people from other generations.** *Do it early and engage both groups. Set expectations about hours of work and work–life balance, frequency and format of coaching/feedback, trust, respect, what's expected with regard to teamwork: 'What do you need me to do to help you?'*

- **engage as many as possible in conversation about generational differences.** *Discuss the generational differences at a comfortable time to highlight why you may be seeing something differently. Involve the quieter people too.*

- **consider working with external support,** *to facilitate open and robust conversations about cross-generational differences.*

- **recognise that there is no quick fix** *and there are no easy answers.*

SUMMARY AND ACTIONS

- There are three generations that currently make up today's workforce: Baby Boomers (born 1946–61); Generation X (Gen X, born 1962–81); and Generation Y (Gen Y, also known as Millennials, born 1982–2001). It is worth noting that Gen Y's successors, Generation Z (Gen Z, born 2002–22), who are quickly approaching employee age, will soon be entering the workforce too.

- Each generation is shaped by different global events that impact the way they view and approach work. There are many inter-generational misunderstandings. These can become opportunities as long as leaders and staff across the different generations are willing to have courageous conversations on generational differences, modify behaviours, seek feedback and learn from these experiences.

Action plan for improving inter-generational connectivity:

- Try to implement two actions from the above list of tips on inter-generation communication within your team/organisation.

- What was the impact?

- What are you learning about how to improve inter-generational communication?

CHAPTER 10

HOW TO CONNECT IN A DIGITAL AGE

The most concerning discrepancies are between the rate in which technology advances, the very slow rate in which adaptive social structures shift in order to accommodate what we know and what we can achieve and the even slower ability to shift our psychology.

Deloitte (2017) 'Rewriting the rules for the digital age'

By now, you should have a better awareness of why connecting with others is vital to our well-being and performing effectively with others. We anticipate that you have an increased awareness of the key blockers for successful connection, an improved self-awareness of your connector type, as well as personal confidence to link up effectively within diverse teams, across various connectors, ages and cultures. When needed, you are also tapping into the RESOLVE model, which will help you handle high-stakes relationships and the seven ways for creating positive connections. However, will the skills of generating positive relationships still be important in a fast-moving digital environment? We would argue that these will become even more valuable in the future.

This chapter will give you the ability to:

- raise your awareness of how technology is changing the way in which we communicate and work with each other and which things will continue to stay the same
- apply tailored tips for each connector type in a digital age that will help you stay connected and keep ahead in a turbulent environment
- apply the RESOLVE framework in a digital world context.

Keep in mind that staying connected is not a one-off but an ongoing process!

TECHNOLOGY IS GROWING FAST

Rapid changes in digital technology are the backdrop against which we will connect with each other in the future. A German high court recently ruled that access to the internet should be considered a basic need. It puts internet access on a par with Maslow's basic needs of food and shelter (Hofstee & Tijmstra, 2019). The United States Organisation for Economic Co-operation and Development (OECD) predicts that, by 2022, each household with 2 children will have around 50 devices with internet connection. This contrasts with today's 10 devices.

Another example of the enormous impact of technology is the growing popularity of the Chinese WeChat, the largest standalone social media and payment application in the world. Currently, it has over one billion users, in line with the Western version (WhatsApp). WeChat (2019) is helping Chinese families and friends to connect with each other and access important health information. It is recognised as being an important vehicle to significantly reduce long queues for goods and services. Payments through the app are both safe and efficient. However, commentators argue that this success carries a potential dark side. Chinese authorities have access to a wealth of personal financial data and, in the future, the government will be able to take decisions about individuals' levels of credit. Furthermore, it has been suggested that the Chinese Government is using the app for mass surveillance on political activists and is censoring sensitive topics. During the COVID-19 pandemic, the use of technology increased exponentially.

TECHNOLOGY IS CHANGING THE WORLD OF WORK

Yuval Harari (2018) argued in his influential book *21 Lessons for the 21st Century* that, by 2050, robots and artificial intelligence (AI) are going to replace humans at work. Harari outlined an inconvenient prediction about the future of work. He claimed that, in order to stay employed, people will continuously have to acquire new relevant skills, and reinvent their professions several times. You may start yourself as a data analyst and, later in life, retrain as a yoga teacher (Harari, 2018). We are already seeing that some of the administrative aspects of legal work jobs (e.g. standard contracts) are being taken over by AI. Innovators in the healthcare sector are guessing that, in the coming years, nurse robots will take control of several mundane aspects of caring for the elderly. It is a likely scenario that self-autonomous cars will replace humans in the next 15 years. Nevertheless, Harari argued that the size and magnitude of the above changes are difficult to predict. It will very much depend on the extent to which governments and politicians allow for this to happen (Harari, 2018).

TECHNOLOGY IS CHANGING RECRUITMENT FOR JOBS

One of the most striking examples of how technology is transforming traditional practices relying on human connections is the recruitment and selection sector.

The multinational Unilever has recently revealed that it uses artificial intelligence (AI) to assess videos of graduates for recruitment purposes (Booth, 2019). The system scans candidates' facial expressions, body language and word choice. The data is then compared with traits that are predictive for job success. Senior executives claim that the recruitment process is less biased, saving 100,000 hours of human recruitment time and £1,000,000 costs. Vodafone, Intel and others are considering similar systems.

Another example of how technology is changing how we recruit people to work is ActiView's system. It utilises a mix of traditional psychology testing with technology. New potential recruits have a virtual tour of the prospective company locations and work virtually through real business challenges. New technology picks up sensory information on each candidate, identifying key attributes, capabilities and drawbacks. Following this, it creates an algorithm, a computer procedure that solves a problem by analysing data through a sequence of specified steps, which then matches the individual talent with the corporate culture and job specification. The algorithm helps to match a suitable candidate profile (based on multiple sources of data including sensory data) with specific companies. It means that recruiters can hire the candidates that are most compatible with the organisation, specific team and position. On the surface, the process of recruitment is done in a bias-free and data-driven approach (see www.actiview.io/). However, the above raises important ethical dilemmas, especially the transparency with the people who own the data on the specific criteria involved. Is it influencing recruitment of a diverse workforce with different backgrounds/ mindsets, rather than homogeneous teams? Furthermore, using sensory data as part of recruitment is highly controversial, and requires further research into the reliability and validity of the technology used as well as an in-depth wider conversation around ethical dilemmas.

HUMAN FACE-TO-FACE COMMUNICATION IS DECLINING

In parallel with the dramatic changes that we are experiencing in the world of work, numerous studies have indicated that the growth in the use of social media is linked to social isolation and the deterioration of our ability to connect in person. Mahmud et al. (2018) showed university students were heavily reliant on social media, which resulted in depression and poor face-to-face communication. The Office for National Statistics in the UK claimed that suicides in females aged 10 to 24 have soared by 83% in six years (Mullin, 2019). One tragic example is Molly Russell (14) who committed suicide in 2017. Her father (Ian) claimed that social media and the companies behind them, such as Facebook, were partly responsible for her death. After this tragic event, the police examined Molly's Instagram account and found distressing material about depression, isolation and suicide (Crawford, 2019). Unfortunately, Molly did not receive the appropriate and timely supportive human connection, which could have prevented this loss. It is an example that mirrors a wealth of emerging data on our dwindling attention span and ability to connect.

OUR ATTENTION SPAN IS DECREASING

In the last 15 years, there is evidence that our attention span has been significantly decreasing from 12 seconds in 2000 to 8 seconds in 2017, resulting in a reduced amount of quality human interaction. Scientists believe that we have shorter attention spans than goldfish, who are able to focus on a task or object for 9 seconds (for further information, visit www.wyzowl.com and search for 'Human attention span'). In a recent workshop, a journalist and editor working at the digital arm of a prestigious organisation said that they are shortening the length of digital articles because of growing evidence that people's attention span is decreasing and they only read the first few paragraphs. It is expected that Generation Z (born 2002–22) will have an even shorter attention span and they will favour the use of technology over face-to-face contact. Ashworth (2019) claimed that technology provides us with updates about members of our network but is less likely to motivate us to connect via a real conversation or in-person meeting. Guy witnessed this phenomenon when challenging his teenage children about reducing the time they spend on social media. In response, they said, 'We look at our iPhone so that we can stay connected with our friends.'

However, other writers such as Caulat (2017) suggested that people using virtual communication can create trust and intimacy with each other. This observation was based on many years of facilitating virtual action learning sets within international companies.

We would concur with her views. Though, in our experience, virtual interaction can be successful on the condition that people had the opportunity to meet in person, to establish trust and connectivity.

Reitz and Higgins (2019), in their book *Speak Up*, claim that when someone is saying that technology is changing everything, try and answer one question, which is 'What do we know won't change?'

OUR NEED TO CONNECT WILL REMAIN STRONG

Although digital technology is becoming much more integral to our lives, Kerr and Levine (2008) argued that we are still highly sensitive to threats of rejection and exclusion from others. As human beings, we hold a tension between our individual goals and inspirations and our need to sustain positive relationships in small groups and get along with others. Guy noticed that his teenage children are linked superficially to many of their peers via social media, but they have a close-knit group of five close friends, with whom they regularly communicate and share intimate information, to support self-esteem and a sense of connection.

Our neural and genetic makeup supports interdependence over independence (Cacioppo, found in Brown, 2018). Siegel (1999) claimed that our mind operates through an integration of thought, feelings, body sensations and logic. When we are in relationships with others, each person is being respected for his/her autonomy and, at the same time, is linked to the other via empathetic communication.

According to Siegel, our connectivity to others is vital for our mental balance, vitality, creativity and harmony. Mike Brent, professor of leadership practise at Hult/Ashridge Executive Education, observed that, despite the increasing use of technology by senior leaders for getting things done, they still require face-to-face interaction with others. This helps them be validated/recognised for their abilities, share/learn from each other across organisational 'silos', and connect emotionally so that they can continue to collaborate and achieve mutually agreed goals. We now turn to look at specific actions/tips for each connector in a digital world.

CONNECTORS IN A DIGITAL AGE

Chapter 3 lays out the basic characteristics of four different connector types. You can identify your personal connector type by visiting https://public.virtual.ashridge.hult.edu/section/connector_type. A hard copy of the connector questionnaire is provided in the Appendix.

See your dominant connector type and specific actions/tips below.

DIRECTOR: GETS THINGS DONE IN A DIGITAL WORLD – YOUR GOAL IS TO BRING OTHER PEOPLE WITH YOU

In the digital age of work, directors will do well to ensure that there is energy and completion around projects. The transactional nature of the workplace will fit into their preference of getting things done. Nevertheless, directors will be required to:

- keep high levels of team morale and engagement by paying extra attention to how you relate to other people
- take time to reflect and improve key relationships
- make sure that the pace of progress is OK for everyone.

FACILITATOR: CREATES HARMONY IN A DIGITAL WORLD – YOUR GOAL IS TO LEARN TO SAY NO

In a digital world, we will probably have more information about people's emotions and agendas via sensors implanted in our body. The experience of being excluded via social media will happen more frequently and much more publicly. In order to survive an increasingly transactional modern world of work, facilitators who thrive on relationships will need to develop a thicker skin so that they can handle the emotional pain arising from much more open conflict and exclusion. At the same time, there will be more lonelier people at work (see data in Chapter 2), and the need for people to connect emotionally with others will expand. Facilitator connector types, with their ability to enhance team well-being and performance, will be in high demand in teams and organisations. However, the tougher and, at times, frosty work environment will require facilitators to:

- be assertive and deal better with conflict
- protect your personal boundaries and say no to requests that are not reasonable. It is important to accept that, on occasion, you will be less liked.

INNOVATOR: MAKES THINGS BETTER IN A DIGITAL WORLD – YOUR GOAL IS TO STAY FOCUSED ON A KEY INNOVATION PROJECT

The changing world of work is heaven for innovators. There will be openness to new ideas/solutions. Nevertheless, innovators will be required to:

- navigate political systems effectively and seek appropriate support for your excellent ideas
- stay focused on a key innovation project and not spread yourself too thinly, resulting in loss of impact and credibility.

SPECIALIST: MAKES THE RIGHT DECISION FOR HIGH QUALITY IN A DIGITAL WORLD – YOUR GOAL IS TO ACCEPT AMBIGUITY AND CHANGE

In a world of fake news and multiple truths, there will be a need for specialists who have expertise in their subject area and are devoted to quality decision making, products and outcomes. Specialists will be required to:

- accept change as part of the new normal at work
- seek good enough quality decisions that will help you and others progress in fast-moving times.

RESOLVE IN A DIGITAL AGE

In Chapter 6, we provided the RESOLVE model to help you turn stressful situations into productive connections. It describes seven tools that enable you to resolve conflict. The RESOLVE model is useful in any context, but we have adapted it specifically to prepare you for the digital age.

The RESOLVE model at a glance:

Realise reality: find clarity in situations and focus on issues that are actually under your control if you have the tendency to get lost within your own thoughts.

Establish clear boundaries: negotiate with clarity and confidence about what is important to you and what are your red lines.

Seek support: elicit the right kind of support because, more often than not, it helps to have at least one person on your side.

Own your part: have the courage to say, 'I am sorry' when and where appropriate. You will be able to acknowledge your strengths as well as your shortcomings.

Listen: open the door to improving your listening skills.

Validate and agree: remember the power of seeing, hearing and understanding someone else's perspective.

Evolve: focus on timing, especially knowing the right time to act.

Step one: Realise reality: find clarity in situations and focus on issues that are actually under your control if you have the tendency to get lost within your own thoughts.

In a work environment, where we are bombarded with emails/ texts with increased pressure/stress and fewer opportunities for face-to-face contact, there is an increased risk for confusion and getting lost in your own fears and, consequently, becoming paralysed. This dynamic is enhanced by the fact that we are disconnected, and lack the information that is naturally present in face-to-face interaction. We tend to compensate on missing information by creating internal stories about the situation.

Key actions for realising reality in a digital era:

- Pick up the phone and/or get connected to distinguish between what is real (information and facts) and what is not (assumptions and fears). In relation to this, notice when you are switching into a 'virtual tour' and are unavailable to respond in the 'here and now'.

- Focus on what is in your control. Nurture key relationships with internal and external stakeholders, including allowing time for face-to-face connection.

- Stay calm and regulate emotions. Try not to get over-emotional and pulled into unnecessary conflict and manipulation.

- Encourage constructive dissent/conflict. Heffernan (2012), in her popular TED talk, discussed the importance of 'daring to disagree'. Digital environments mean that leaders can stick to emails and avoid direct conversation/healthy conflict on what's important for the success of the organisation. She encourages leaders to promote constructive debate and ensure that they have people around them who are able and willing to challenge their views. Heffernan warns against the phenomena of having eco-chambers and sameness of views in organisations. Instead, she believes in diverse view mindsets to support learning and innovation.

Step two: Establish clear boundaries – negotiate with clarity and confidence about what is important to you and what are your red lines.

In a digital world where communication tends to be transactional (e.g. email/WhatsApp), it may be much more difficult to have robust conversation on personal red lines.

Key actions for establishing clear boundaries in a digital age:

- Stay connected with key relationships regularly. If there is a problem, pick up the phone and/or meet face to face. Virtual communication is not a substitute for connecting with others face to face, noticing and responding to others' emotions/body language which can give you important clues about what they really need and want.

- A digital environment creates more work pressure and it's OK to say no. One of the traps of high-performing managers is saying yes to too many requests. This results in burn-out and derailment. Learn to be approachable yet firm. It's important that others know your limits/boundaries and what is acceptable behaviour and what's not. In this process, it is crucial to realise that there is no need for you to be loved by others. Instead, we encourage you to hold onto your personal/professional lines. As one managing director told us, 'If you want to be loved, buy a puppy'.

Step three: Seek support – elicit the right kind of support because, more often than not, it helps to have at least one person on your side.

In a demanding digital world, with 24/7 access to information and increased pressure on short-term targets, there will be increased loneliness. Furthermore, with the rise of volatility in the working environment, there will be a need to contain ambiguity and take on more risks, which, subsequently, can lead to personal failures. In this context, taking care of oneself is becoming a necessity rather than a nice to have.

Key actions for seeking support in a digital age:

- Leverage on technology to seek support from others. For example, you can seek and provide regular consultation from people all over the world.
- Stay connected with friends, colleagues and support groups.

Step four: Own your part – have the courage to say, 'I am sorry' when and where appropriate. You will be able to acknowledge your strengths as well as your shortcomings.

In a digital world of work where people have little span of attention, it's easy to blame others for your own mistakes. However, Tang (2019) argued that you should not hesitate and/or be ashamed to own your mistakes. It's important to recognise that you are human.

Key actions for owning your part in a digital era:

- Take personal responsibility for your online presence.
- In a digital age, we are bombarded with information and it's easy to get distracted. We worked with a manager who bragged that he can play video games while participating in important business meetings online. He said, 'I only need to shut down the

video games audio.' Overcome the temptation to multitask just because others can't see what you are doing. Be accountable for your own presence.

- Whether it's face to face or emails/WhatsApp, be prepared to acknowledge courageously the other person's emotions and take responsibility for your actions/misunderstandings: 'I am really sorry that you feel this way, it was not my intention'; 'I understand my part in this problem'.

Step five: Listen – open the door to improving your listening skills.

Listening is a major tool in creating and maintaining human relationships. In the digital era, it's especially challenging due to the lack of access to feedback that we naturally receive through body language. Through text messaging, email, audio calls, or even video conferencing, the communication becomes two-dimensional and flat.

Key actions for listening in the digital era:

- The virtual environment calls for people to ask for explicit feedback, in order to compensate for missing out on our natural ability to read body language and the emotional atmosphere in the room.
- Be mindful of emojis and what they are conveying.
- Be prepared to invest the extra energy required when listening via a virtual medium.

Step six: Validate and agree – remember the power of seeing, hearing and understanding someone else's perspective.

Here, we recommend that we use compassion to overcome disagreements and move successfully forward. Amy Bradley, a writer and consultant, argued in her recent book *The Human Moment* that compassion is a core human activity that is ignored in the business world. Jeff Weiner, CEO of LinkedIn (2019), has introduced the concept of compassionate management within the organisation. He argued that compassion can progress organisational culture and performance.

Key actions for validating in a digital era:

- Use technology as an enabler to increase the ability to see the world from others' points of view though online conversations with people living in different geographies.

- Use virtual platforms to engage and hear the diversity of views among your employees, and aim to foster kindness and willingness to support others who may have a different point of view from yourself.

Step seven: Evolve: focus on timing, epecially knowing the right time to act.

Relationships are dynamic and we continuously need to evolve into the next level of joint working.

Key actions for evolving in a digital era:

- Understand that power is more pronounced in a digital age. Few people will hold power and access to data and information. Here, there is no 'quick fix'. Evolving requires being aware of power dynamics.

- Reposition yourself by connecting to others. There is a power in numbers and our access to technology also opens the opportunity to connect across borders and cultures.

- Decide what's achievable in this business relationship and whether it is worthwhile to pursue as a connection or terminate the relationship. Do not give up on difficult conversations and go the extra mile and create the space for personal meetings.

SUMMARY AND ACTIONS

- Technology is impacting all spheres of our lives.
- The digital age has provided us with many advantages and, at the same time, we are witnessing a reduction in human connection and an increase in loneliness.
- Nevertheless, our need for connection remains strong and the skills for creating effective relationships are becoming much more invaluable.

GET CONNECTED NOW

You have already taken a significant first step by reading this book. The next phase is to deepen your connection to yourself and others. This requires challenging old patterns and having a courageous and honest look in the mirror.

Ask yourself:

- Can you find the space to meet yourself with compassion, and soften your inner critic?
- Can you add to your busy schedule a meeting with you?
- Can you say no to being overworked and overwhelmed?
- Would you allow the grind of the day-to-day schedule to prevent you from taking time to engage and nurture strategic collaborations?
- Would you commit to having a difficult conversation with a colleague on mutual expectations?
- Would you take the risk and deepen your relationship rather than shy away and keep the relationship at a superficial level?
- Would you have the courage to show up?

The answers lie within you. Getting connected to oneself and others is a matter of choice reflected in your routine activities and how you decide to spend your time. Your calendar reveals your true priorities.

Being connected is an imperative of being more effective and happier. *The time to do it is now!*

APPENDIX

CONNECTOR QUESTIONNAIRE

The 'Connector Type' tool assists an individual in understanding their own behaviour as well as becoming empathic to others. It helps to connect to others in a deeper and more meaningful way. The ability to be aware of oneself is the path to freedom and choice. When you become aware of your connector type and its impact on others, you can start modifying your behaviour to get the result you are looking for. This kind of understanding opens the door to connect and respond in a manner that is much more productive and impactful for achieving collaboration and mutually agreed goals.

Listed below are different ways in which you might behave, act and communicate. In the following sets of 4 statements, please distribute a total of 10 points between the statements. Please always use all 10 points between the items. You may use zeros if you feel they are appropriate.

Here's an example: distribute 10 points between the items with regard to how they correspond to you:

I analyse all potential outcomes before making a decision	8
I let my 'gut feeling' make my decisions	0
I make decisions depending on how practical they are	1
I believe the best decisions will be made when you are spontaneous	1

Total: 10

Distribute all 10 points between the Items with regard to how they correspond:

1. to you when you need to solve a problem

I act impulsively	
I collect data and am very calculated in the way I solve problems	
I focus on finding the most effective way to solve the problem; I appreciate predictability	
I look for solutions that would meet people's needs	

2. to you when you communicate

When I communicate, I tend to get right to the point	
Before I form an opinion, I want to have as much information as I can	
In a meeting, it is important to me that everybody has time to express themselves	
I think about several ideas at the same time and dialogue with others helps me sharpen my ideas	

3. to you when you are dealing with new ideas

I judge ideas by how practical they are	
I have an innovating mind and seek new ideas and perspective	
I am analytically minded	
When coming up with ideas, it is important to me that they take into consideration how people feel and that the ideas benefit the entire team	

4. to what you find important at work

To get the job done	
The space to use my skills and expertise	
The ability to think about new ideas outside the box	
People's happiness and satisfaction	

Distribute all 10 points between the items with regard to how they correspond:

5. to how you perceive work-related conflicts

I avoid conflicts to create harmony in the team	
I am happy with conflicts that support new ideas	
I want conflicts to be resolved quickly in order to complete the task	
I believe conflicts can be useful when they are based on facts instead of emotions	

6. to how you are

I am self-sufficient and like to take charge of situations	
I am at my best when provided with information	
I am considered to be a people person	
I thrive on tackling new challenges	

7. to your working style

I tend to be direct and to the point	
My preference is to listen to various viewpoints and make informed decisions	
I am sensitive towards my co-workers' feelings	
I am spontaneous and flexible	

8. to what you value at work

Efficiency is important to me	
Having space to think and express myself	
I value objectivity and data	
I value relationships	

Distribute all 10 points between the items with regard to how they correspond:

9. to how you find meetings with co-workers

I prefer meetings that are direct, efficient and to the point	
I believe in stretching what is possible in order to create something new	
I prefer meetings that have robust content and follow a logical process	
In a meeting, I first want to make people feel comfortable	

10. to your personal drivers

Outputs of high standard	
Intuition and creativity	
To use your knowledge and expertise	
To engage with other people's opinions	

11. to how you deal with change in the workplace

I accept the change if there is a clear purpose with the initiative	
I accept the change as long as it brings safety and harmony to people around me	
I actively seek change opportunities in the workplace	
I accept change if I can contribute with my expertise	

12. to your perceived strengths

I am good at contributing with innovative ideas	
I am reliable in terms of getting things done	
I am good at contributing with knowledge and facts	
I am good at creating a positive work environment	

Distribute all 10 points between the items with regard to how they correspond:

13. to your goals at work

My goal at work is to produce high-quality work	
My goal at work is to contribute with new ways of thinking/working	
My goal at work is to get work done	
My goal at work is to create harmony among people	

14. to what triggers stress

Unresolved work conflicts	
Resolving problems that are outside of my expertise	
Slow and inefficient work	
Little opportunity to contribute ideas to projects and an emphasis on keeping to deadlines	

15. to how you find informal work events (such as workplace events, dinners or drinks)

I like to get to know more about my colleagues	
I find them a waste of time unless they lead to productive outcomes	
I like to share my ideas to a wider audience	
I like to stick to conversations that involve my expertise	

SCORING SHEET

DIRECTOR

1c + 2a + 3a + 4a + 5c + 6a + 7b + 8a + 9a + 10a + 11a + 12b + 13c + 14c + 15b =

FACILITATOR

1d + 2c + 3d + 4d + 5a + 6c + 7a + 8d + 9d + 10d + 11b + 12d + 13d + 14a + 15a =

INNOVATOR

1a + 2d + 3b + 4c + 5b + 6d + 7c + 8b + 9b + 10b + 11c + 12a + 13b + 14d + 15c =

SPECIALIST

1b + 2b + 3c + 4b + 5d + 6b + 7d + 8c + 9c + 10c + 11d + 12c + 13a + 14b + 15d =

DIRECTOR CONNECTOR TYPE

Basic motive: to achieve the goal. The director is motivated by the need to 'make things happen'.

Main strategy: control.

Characteristics: they like to organise projects, operations, procedures and people. They are determined and like to act and get things done. They live by a set of clear standards and beliefs, make a systematic effort to follow these, and expect the same of others. They value competence and efficiency. Directors enjoy interacting and working with others as long as they are responsible about meeting deadlines and completing assigned tasks. People with a dominant director type feel comfortable with planned change, structure and predictability.

Strengths: they usually have a strong presence. They are reliable and consistent. They usually are competent and are knowledgeable about finding the information that they need. Most of them look confident regardless of how they feel.

Challenges: they may struggle to deal with emergent and unexpected change. Directors have little patience with confusion, inefficiency and halfway measures. Many of them find it difficult to express emotions and be vulnerable. They operate under a lot of 'should'.

Triggers: they are confused when others express emotions. They are triggered by situations where they perceive they have no control. They are triggered when things are not done the way in which they believe things should be done.

In meetings: they are focused on outcomes and high energy. They prefer a structured agenda with each agenda item being discussed and with follow-up actions with specific timelines and action items for each team member. They are extremely annoyed with small talk which they deem a waste of time and resources.

Decision making: this is both fast and expedient and they may view the consensus-building process as a waste of time. They like to depend on data but don't want to have too much of it. They usually evaluate ideas based on an objective criterion which heavily relies on how practical these are in practice.

Change: they don't like change but are willing to change if they understand the purpose and the destination.

FACILITATOR CONNECTOR TYPE

Basic motive: to create harmony.

Main strategy: being attuned and attentive to other people's needs.

Characteristics: they are highly empathetic and attuned to others, compassionate and use their EQ (emotional intelligence) to quickly understand emotional needs, motivations and concerns. They can be inspiring leaders as well as good team members who maintain harmony. Facilitators are interested in relationships and have a good understanding of how groups and individuals work. They are natural mediators. Facilitators are adaptable and like variety and new challenges. They are exceptionally insightful into possibilities. When change is introduced, their main concern is how it will impact relationships. When communicating, they tend to listen to and support others but also have definite values and opinions of their own. They bring enthusiasm and intensity to creating strong relationships. Others view facilitators as sociable and with a large circle of friends. They value authentic and intimate relationships and, at times, will take on other people's emotions and work, which may result in burn-out and stress.

Strengths: they are good listeners, attentive and loyal to the people they are close to. They value people over outcomes. They are sociable and value others.

Challenges: they are sensitive and vulnerable. They can lose sight of the goal and they have difficulty saying no.

Triggers: being sensitive, they have thin skin and have a tendency to get hurt easily.

In meetings: they are warm and friendly. Facilitators want to make sure that everyone has the opportunity to express themselves. They are motivated by being liked and are in need of approval from others. Facilitators take responsibility for organising interactions with colleagues, friends or family so that all are involved. They prefer a collaborative and engaged decision-making process and prize harmony and cooperation. Feelings guide their decision making rather than rationale thinking and data. They are happy to support other people's ideas; in particular, when they can see social benefits for the team/organisation or the wider world.

Decision making: they are slow to make decisions. They prefer to listen to different opinions before making decisions. They need to have a quiet space in order to be able to hear their own voice.

Change: they are usually not resistant to change but need time to adjust. A gentle and soft environment is helpful for them.

INNOVATOR CONNECTOR TYPE

Basic motive: to make things better, to improve and change.

Main strategy: they love complex challenges and readily synthesise complicated, theoretical and abstract matters. They have global thinking and dreams for the future. Innovators are focused on visionary ideas and concepts. They are independent problem solvers and are comfortable in change, ambiguity and exploration.

Characteristics: they usually have high energy and are often restless. Many of them appear as day dreamers but, once they have created their general structure, they devise strategies to achieve their ambitious goals. Their plans can be complex and are not always very practical. They are capable of mobilising resources to make these ideas happen. Innovators thrive on change/ambiguity and are comfortable with emergent plans.

Strengths: they are dreamers, the people that are often ahead of their time. They have a unique way of thinking and their passion is often contentious. They are quick thinkers.

Challenges: they have difficulty with practicalities. Most of them are allergic to forms and bureaucracy. They have a tendency to break the rules and, as a result, they get in trouble in organisations. They are often distracted and find it a challenge to follow through.

Triggers: routine.

In meetings: they express creative ideas, innovate, generate excitement and 'outside of the box' thinking. Innovators are restless and willing to challenge the status quo. Their presentation is ever changing, they can appear logical and rational and, a minute later, they can embark on a vision that seems completely out of touch. They struggle with a structured agenda and will tend to jump from one topic on the agenda to another.

Decision making: when making decisions, their focus is on big ideas. They do not like long decision-making processes or discussions on minor/ mundane issues. They prefer integrated decision making, drawing on various aspects/areas. They will get bored by following through on actions. They may find it difficult to follow up on issues/actions and do not like details and mundane tasks.

Change: they seek change even though they often feel tired by their own pace.

SPECIALIST CONNECTOR TYPE

Basic motive: to make the right decision, the right move.

Main strategy: move slowly, collect data and avoid making mistakes.

Characteristics: they are practical, sensible and realistic. They have a strong sense of responsibility and great loyalty to their organisations. Specialists are dependable and interested in applying their knowledge and expertise. They will do what is necessary in order to perform their job correctly and achieve a high-quality outcome. Most of them have a tendency to be introverted. Specialists prefer to work alone and be accountable for the results within an environment where both jobs and roles are clearly defined. Creativity is not an area of strength, but they will be happy to support others with innovative ideas/projects provided enough data/facts rationale is provided.

Strengths: systematic, reliable and knowledgeable.

Challenges: they have a tendency to overthink. Many of them experience communication problems. They have difficulty making their voice heard.

Triggers: when they are required to process a lot of information quickly, and when they don't have time to process and collect what they perceive are enough data to make a decision. They fear making mistakes and are terrified when they feel judged.

In meetings: they talk when asked. They take time to reflect before talking. They will use logic, relevant content and data in their arguments. They will come across as careful as they thoroughly apply a logical criterion based on their experience and knowledge. They are more comfortable providing input on their area of expertise rather than on general strategic areas. Specialists do not like 'small talk'. They are perceived as consistent and orderly and run meetings accordingly.

Decision making: when making decisions, they will want decisions to be grounded in both data and expertise.

Change: they prefer predictable change, which allows them to bring their expertise into play. They are not interested in change for change's sake. They will support change only when facts demonstrate that such change will bring better results.

REFERENCES

CHAPTER 1

Ainsworth, M.D.S. (1973) 'The development of infant-mother attachment'.
In Caldwell, B. and Ricciuti, H. (eds.) *Review of Child Development
Research* (Vol. 3, pp. 1–94). Chicago: University of Chicago Press.

Bowlby, J. (1969) *Attachment. Attachment and Loss: Vol. 1. Loss*. New
York: Basic Books.

Brown, B. (2018) *Dare to Lead*. New York: Random House.

Cacioppo, J. (2018) See www.nytimes.com/2018/03/26/obituaries/john-
cacioppo-who-studied-effects-of-loneliness-is-dead-at-66.html.

Gentry, B. (2016) Center for Creative Leadership (Bill Gentry blog).
Available at: www.ccl.org/blog/5-warning-signs-new-experienced-
leaders-derailing/.

Global Catastrophic Risks, see: http://globalprioritiesproject.org/wp-content/
uploads/2016/04/Global-Catastrophic-Risk-Annual-Report-2016-FINAL.pdf.

Hogan, R. (2007) *Personality and the Fate of Organizations*. Mahwah, NJ:
Lawrence Erlbaum.

Lieberman, M.D. (2015) *Social: Why Our Brains Are Wired to Connect*.
Oxford: Oxford University Press.

Mamo, E. (2018) 'How to combat the rise of workplace loneliness'.
Report. Available at: www.totaljobs.com/insidejob/how-to-combat-
the-rise-of-workplace-loneliness/.

Maslow, A.H. (1943) 'A theory of human motivation', *Psychological
Review*, 50(4), 370–96.

Raquepaw, J.M. and Miller, R.S. (1989) 'Psychotherapist burnout:
A componential analysis', *Professional Psychology: Research and
Practice*, 20(1), 32–6.

Rock, D. (2008) 'SCARF: a brain-based model for collaborating with and
influencing others', *NeuroLeadership Journal*, issue one.

Shipman, P. (2010) 'The animal connection and human evolution',
Current Anthropology, 51(4), 519–38.

CHAPTER 2

Anthony, S.D. (2016) 'Kodak's downfall wasn't about technology',
Harvard Business Review, 15 July. Available at: https://hbr.
org/2016/07/kodaks-downfall-wasnt-about-technology.

Arnsten, A.F.T. (1998) 'The biology of being frazzled', *Science*. 280, 1711–2.

Barr, S. (2018) 'More than half of lonely adults fear no one will notice if something bad happens to them', *Independent*, 26 November. Available at: www.independent.co.uk/life-style/health-and-families/loneliness-adults-fear-isolation-social-connections-uk-red-cross-survey-a8652061.html.

Barford, V. (2013) 'Is modern life making us lonely?' *BBC News Magazine*, 8 April. Available at: www.bbc.co.uk/news/magazine-22012957.

Care Quality Commission. Available at: www.cqc.org.uk/guidance-providers/all-services/success-factor-1-committed-leadership#culture.

Cook, M. (1998) *Personnel Selection: Adding Value Through People*. New York: Wiley.

Edmondson, A.C. (2012) *Teaming – How Organizations Learn, Innovate, and Compete in the Knowledge Economy*. San Francisco: Jossey-Bass.

Fillingham, D. and Weir, B. (2014) 'System leadership: Lessons and learning from AQuA's Integrated Care Discovery Communities', The King's Fund. Available at: www.kingsfund.org.uk/sites/default/files/field/field_publication_file/system-leadership-october-2014.pdf.

Fredrickson, B.L. (2001) 'The role of positive emotions in positive psychology: the broaden and build theory of positive emotions', *American Psychologist*, 56, 218–26.

Gordon, E. (2000) *Integrative Neuroscience: Bringing Together Biological, Psychological and Clinical Models of the Human Brain*. Singapore: Harwood Academic Publishers.

Harter, J. (2018) 'Employee engagement on the rise in the U.S.', 26 August. Available at: https://news.gallup.com/poll/241649/employee-engagement-rise.aspx.

Honoré, S. and Paine Schofield, C. (2012) 'Culture shock: Generation Y and their managers around the World', Ashridge Business School Research Centre. Available at: www.researchgate.net/profile/Carina_Paine_Schofield/publication/328964800.

Janis, I.L. (1982) *Groupthink*. Second edition. Boston, MA: Wadsworth, Cengage Learning.

Linder, J.C., Cross, R. and Parker, A. (2006) 'All charged up', *Business Strategy Review*, 17(3), 25–9.

McCord, P. (2014) 'How Netflix reinvented HR', *Harvard Business Review*, January–February.

Mehrabian, A. (1981) *Silent Messages: Implicit Communication of Emotions and Attitudes*. Belmont, CA: Wadsworth.

Mitchell, J.P. Macrae, C.N. and Banaji, M.R. (2006) 'Dissociable medial prefrontal contributions to judgments of similar and dissimilar others', *Neuron*, 50, 655–63.

Munch, D. (2017) 'Why middle managers are the key to quality improvement success', Institute for Healthcare Improvement. Available at: www.ihi.org/communities/blogs/why-middle-managers-are-the-key-to-qi-success.

Norton, S. (2015) 'Mindfulness meditation is big business in London's square mile', *Independent*, 14 March. Available at: www.independent.co.uk/life-style/health-and-families/features/mindfulness-meditation-is-big-business-in-londons-square-mile-10100970.html.

Oshry, B. (1999) *Leading Systems – Lessons from the Power Lab*. San Francisco: Berrett-Koehler Publishers.

Peters, S. (2012) *The Chimp Paradox: The Mind Management Programme for Confidence, Success and Happiness*. London: Vermilion.

Phelps, E.A. (2006) 'Emotion and cognition. Insights from studies of the human amygdala', *Annual Review of Psychology*, 57, 27–53.

Reynolds, A. and Lewis, D. (2017) 'Closing the strategy-execution gap means focusing on what employees think, not what they do', *Harvard Business Review*, 30 October. Available at: https://hbr.org/2017/10/closing-the-strategy-execution-gap-means-focusing-on-what-employees-think-not-what-they-do.

Robinson, N. (2012) 'Former RBS boss Fred Goodwin stripped of knighthood', BBC News, 31 January. Available at: www.bbc.co.uk/news/uk-politics-16821650.

Rock, D. (2008) 'SCARF: a brain-based model for collaborating with and influencing others', *NeuroLeadership Journal*, issue one.

Schawbel, D. (2018) *Back to Human: How Great Leaders Create Connection in the Age of Isolation*. London: Piatkus.

Schein, E.H. (2017) *Organizational Culture and Leadership*. Fifth edition. Hoboken, NJ: Wiley.

Schwartz, J. and Wald, M.L. (2003) 'The nation: NASA's curse?; "Groupthink" is 30 years old, and still going strong', *The New York Times*, 9 March. Available at: www.nytimes.com/2003/03/09/weekinreview/the-nation-nasa-s-curse-groupthink-is-30-years-old-and-still-going-strong.html.

Singer, T., Seymour, B., O'Doherty, J.P., Stephan, K.E., Dolan, R.J. and Frith, C.D. (2006) 'Empathetic neural responses are modulated by the perceived fairness of others', *Nature*, 439, 466–9.

Syed, M. (2016) *Black Box Thinking: Marginal Gains and the Secrets of High Performance*. London: John Murray.

Vasel, K. (2018) 'Why workplace loneliness is bad for business', CNN Business, 5 December. Available at: https://edition.cnn.com/2018/12/05/success/workplace-loneliness/index.html.

West, M. (2018) 'It's not about the money: staff engagement comes first', The King's Fund. Available at: www.kingsfund.org.uk/blog/2018/03/staff-engagement-comes-first.

Wiggins, L. and Hunter, H. (2016) *Relational Change: The Art and Practice of Changing Organizations*. London: Bloomsbury.

Yohn, D.L. (2017) 'Here's who is stalling your culture efforts', SmartBrief, 17 March. Available at: www.smartbrief.com/original/2017/03/heres-who-stalling-your-culture-efforts.

Zak, P.J., Kurzban, R. and Matzner, W.T. (2005) 'Oxytocin is associated with human trustworthiness', *Hormones and Behaviour*, 48(5), 522–7.

Zenger, J. and Folkman, J. (2014) 'Why middle managers are so unhappy', *Harvard Business Review*, 24 November. Available at: https://hbr.org/2014/11/why-middle-managers-are-so-unhappy.

CHAPTER 3

Hoffman, E. (2002) *Psychological Testing at Work: How to Use, Interpret, and Get the Most Out of the Newest Tests in Personality, Learning Styles, Aptitudes, Interests, and More*. New York: McGraw-Hill.

Hogan, R. (2007) *Personality and the Fate of Organizations*. Mahwah, NJ: Lawrence Erlbaum.

Jung, C. (1921) *Psychological Types*. Available at: www.123test.com/jung-typology/.

CHAPTER 4

Boaz, N. and Fox, E.A. (2014) 'Change leader, change thyself', *McKinsey Quarterly,* March.

Cohen, A.R. and Bradford, D.L. (2005) *Influence Without Authority*. Hoboken, NJ: Wiley.

Heffernan, M. (2012) 'Dare to disagree'. TED talk. Available at: www.ted.com/talks/margaret_heffernan_dare_to_disagree.

Owen, J. (2018) *How to Lead*. Fifth edition. Harlow: Pearson.

Robertson, P. (2005) 'Always change a winning team'. *Marshall Cavendish Business*, 24 January. Available at: https://papers.ssrn.com/sol3/papers.cfm?abstract_id=2191887.

CHAPTER 5

Binney, G., Wilke, G. and Williams, C. (2009) *Living Leadership: A Practical Guide for Ordinary Heroes*. Second edition. Harlow: FT Prentice Hall.

Cooper, C., Flint-Taylor, J. and Pearn, M. (2013) *Building Resilience for Success. A Resource for Managers and Organizations*. Basingstoke: Palgrave Macmillan.

Csikszentmihalyi, M. (2007) *Finding Flow: The Psychology of Engagement with Everyday Life*. New York: Basic Books.

Doz, Y. and Kosonen, M. (2008) 'The dynamics of strategic agility: Nokia's rollercoaster experience', *California Management Review*, 50(3), 95–118.

Furnham, A. (2013) 'The dark side of leadership management derailment', EAWOP conference talk. Available at: www.eawop.org/ckeditor_assets/attachments/416/worklab_2013_adrianfurnham_talk2.pdf?1384979822.

Gentry, B. (2016) 'The 5 warning signs that new (and experienced) leaders are derailing', Center for Creative Leadership (Bill Gentry blog). Available at: www.ccl.org/blog/5-warning-signs-new-experienced-leaders-derailing/.

Kets de Vries, M.F.R. (2006) *The Leader on the Couch: A Clinical Approach to Changing People and Organizations*. San Francisco, CA: Jossey-Bass.

Lombardo, M.L. and Eichinger, R.W. (1989) *Preventing Derailment: What to Do Before it's Too Late*. Greensboro, NC: Center for Creative Leadership.

Reitz, M. and Higgins, J. (2019) *Speak Up*. Harlow: Pearson.

Tang, A. (2019) *The Leader's Guide to Mindfulness: How to Use Soft Skills to Get Hard Results*. Harlow: Pearson.

Zak, P.J. (2017) 'The neuroscience of trust: Management behaviors that foster employee engagement', *Harvard Business Review*, January–February. Available at: https://hbr.org/2017/01/the-neuroscience-of-trust.

CHAPTER 6

ABC (2011) *Oprah Winfrey Show*, 25 May. Chicago, USA.

Becker-Phelps, L. (2019) 'Don't believe everything you think', *Psychology Today*, 8 July. Available at: www.psychologytoday.com/gb/blog/making-change/201907/dont-believe-everything-you-think.

Covey, S.R. (2005) *The 7 Habits of Highly Effective People*. New York: Simon & Schuster.

Giles, L. (2013) *Sun Tzu On The Art of War*. Abingdon: Routledge.

Harvard Business Review on Lars Sørensen (2015) 'The Best-Performing CEOs in the World', *Harvard Business Review*. Available at: https://hbr.org/2015/11/the-best-performing-ceos-in-the-world.

McKay, M., Davis, M. and Fanning, P. (2009) *Messages: The Communication Skills Book*. Third edition. Oakland, CA: New Harbinger Publications.

Niebuhr, R. (n.d.) 'The Serenity Prayer: What Does it Mean?' Celebrate Recovery. Available at: https://www.celebraterecovery.com/resources/cr-tools/serenityprayer.

Werner, E.E. (2005) 'What can we learn about resilience from large-scale longitudinal studies?' In Goldstein, S. and Brooks, R.B. (eds) *Handbook of Resilience in Children* (pp. 91–105). New York: Kluwer.

Williamson, M. (1992) *A Return to Love: Reflections on the Principles of 'A Course in Miracles'*. New York: HarperCollins.

CHAPTER 7

Clifton, J. (2017) 'The world's broken workplace', Gallup, 13 June. Available at: https://news.gallup.com/opinion/chairman/212045/world-broken-workplace.aspx.

Edmondson, A.C. (2019) *The Fearless Organization: Creating Psychological Safety in the Workplace for Learning, Innovation, and Growth*. Hoboken, NJ: Wiley.

Hickson, G.B., Clayton, F.W., Githens, P.B. and Sloan, F.A. (1992) 'Factors that prompted families to file medical malpractice claims following perinatal injuries', *Journal of the American Medical Association*, 267(10), 1359–63.

Horsager, D. (2012) *The Trust Edge: How Top Leaders Gain Faster Results, Deeper Relationships, and a Stronger Bottom Line*. New York: Free Press.

Nelson, P. (2013) *Autobiography in Five Short Chapters*. Louisville: Contre Coup Press.

Parker, N. (2013) 'The Angel in the Marble: Modern life lessons from history's greatest sculptor', July 9. Available at: https://medium.com/@nilsaparker/the-angel-in-the-marble-f7aa43f333dc.

Rosenthal, R. and Jacobson, L. (1992) *Pygmalion in the Classroom: Teacher Expectation and Pupils' Intellectual Development*. Bancyfelin, Carmarthen: Crown House Publishing.

Scott, K.M. (2017) *Radical Candor: Be a Kickass Boss Without Losing Your Humanity*. New York: St. Martin's Press.

Treasurer, B. (2019) *Courage Goes To Work: How to Build Backbones, Boost Performance, and Get Results*. San Francisco: Berrett-Koehler Publishers.

CHAPTER 8

Adler N.J. (2001) *Boston to Beijing: Managing with a World View*. First edition. Mason, OH: South-Western/Thomson Learning.

BBC News (2000) 'GlaxoSmithKline gets US merger approval', 18 December. Available at: http://news.bbc.co.uk/1/hi/business/1076000.stm.

Cable, D. (2018) 'How humble leadership really works', *Harvard Business Review*, 23 April. Available at: https://hbr.org/2018/04/how-humble-leadership-really-works.

Ferrell, O.C, Fraedrich, J. and Ferrell, L. (2011) *Business Ethic: Ethical Decision Making and Cases*. Ninth edition. Mason, OH: South Western Cengage Learning.

Fuchs, B., Reitz, M. and Higgins, J. (2018) 'Do you have "Advantage Blindness"?' *Harvard Business Review*, 10 April. Available at: https://hbr.org/2018/04/do-you-have-advantage-blindness.

Goleman, D. (1996) *Emotional Intelligence: Why It Can Matter More Than IQ*. New York: Bantam.

Hofstede, G., Hofstede, G.J. and Minkov, M. (2010) *Cultures and Organizations: Software of the Mind: Intercultural Cooperation and its Importance for Survival*. New York: McGraw-Hill.

Liswood, L. (2010) *The Loudest Duck: Moving Beyond Diversity while Embracing Differences to Achieve Success at Work*. Hoboken, NJ: John Wiley.

Reddy, B. (1994) *Intervention Skills*. New York: Wiley.

Sadtler, D., Smith, D. and Campbell, A. (2008) *Smarter Acquisitions: Ten Steps to Successful Deals*. Harlow: Pearson.

Zak, P.J. (2017) 'The neuroscience of trust', *Harvard Business Review*, January–February. Available at: https://hbr.org/2017/01/the-neuroscience-of-trust.

CHAPTER 9

Cotton, B. (2019) '2020 workforce to be dominated by Millennials', *Business Leader*, 7 January. Available at: www.businessleader.co.uk/2020-workforce-to-be-dominated-by-millennials/57878/.

Honoré, S., Brown, G. and Paine Schofield, C. (2017) 'The voice of the Baby Boomers, changing the workplace for the future', Ashridge Executive Education, Hult International Business School report.

Honoré, S. and Paine Schofield, C. (2012) 'Generation Y and their managers around the world', Ashridge Business School report.

Office for National Statistics (ONS) (2015) 'UK Labour Market: July 2015', *Statistical Bulletin*, 15 July. Available at: www.ons.gov.uk/ons/dcp171778_408140.pdf.

Office for National Statistics (ONS) (2018) 'How do the post-World War baby boom generations compare?', 6 March. Available at: www.ons.gov.uk/peoplepopulationandcommunity/birthsdeathsandmarriages/ageing/articles/howdothepostworldwarbabyboomgenerationscompare/2018-03-06.

Paine Schofield, C. and Franze, L. (2011) 'Great expectations: managing Generation Y', Institute of Leadership and Management and Ashridge Business School report.

Paine Schofield, C. and Honoré, S. (2015) 'Don't put Baby (Boomers) in the corner: realising the potential of the over 50s at work', Ashridge Business School report.

CHAPTER 10

Ashworth, C. (2019) 'Are we losing the human connection?', *Forbes*, 1 August. Available at: www.forbes.com/sites/forbeshumanresourcescouncil/2019/08/01/are-we-losing-the-human-connection/.

Booth, R. (2019) 'Unilever saves on recruiters by using AI to assess job interviews', *The Guardian*, 25 October. Available at: www.theguardian.com/technology/2019/oct/25/unilever-saves-on-recruiters-by-using-ai-to-assess-job-interviews.

Bradley, A. (2019) *The Human Moment: The Positive Power of Compassion in the Workplace*. London: LID Publishing.

Brown, B. (2018) *Dare to Lead*. New York: Random House.

Caulat, G. (2017) 'Virtual Action Learning: A new genre for powerful learning', *The Future of Learning*. Available at: https://link.springer.com/chapter/10.1057/9780230306356_7.

Crawford, A. (2019) 'Instagram "helped kill my daughter"', BBC News, 22 January. Available at: www.bbc.co.uk/news/av/uk-46966009/instagram-helped-kill-my-daughter.

Deloitte. (2017) 'Rewriting the rules for the digital age'. Available at: https://www2.deloitte.com/content/dam/Deloitte/global/Documents/HumanCapital/hc-2017-global-human-capital-trends-gx.pdf.

Harari, Y.N. (2018) *21 Lessons for the 21st Century*. New York: Vintage.

Heffernan, M. (2012) 'Dare to disagree'. TED talk. Available at: https://www.ted.com/talks/margaret_heffernan_dare_to_disagree.

Hofstee, G. and Tijmstra, S. (2019) *Business Strategy Through Disruption*. The Hague: Uitgeverij U2pi BV.

Hogan (2017) 'Strategies to help teams achieve full potential', Team Report Technical Manual. Available at: www.hoganteamreport.com/wp-content/uploads/sites/10/2017/01/Team_Report_Tech_Manual_V2.pdf.

Kerr, N.L. and Levine, J.M. (2008) 'The detection of social exclusion: Evolution and beyond', *Group Dynamics: Theory, Research, and Practice*, 12(1), 39–52.

Mahmud, M.M., Ramachandiran, C.R. and Ismail, O. (2018) 'Social media dependency: The implications of technological communication use among university students' in Tang, S.F. and Cheah, S.E. (eds.) *Redesigning Learning for Greater Social impact*, pp. 71–87. New York: Springer.

Mullin, G. (2019) 'Suicide rates in girls soar 83% with those as young as TEN taking their lives', *The Sun*, 3 September. Available at: www.thesun.co.uk/news/9851546/child-suicide-death-rates-soar/.

Reitz, M. and Higgins, J. (2019) *Speak Up*. Harlow: Pearson.

Siegel, D.J. (1999) 'About interpersonal neurobiology'. Available at: www.drdansiegel.com/about/interpersonal_neurobiology/.

Tang, A. (2019) *The Leader's Guide to Mindfulness: How to Use Soft Skills to Get Hard Results*. Harlow: Pearson.

WeChat (2019) 'How to use WeChat and QQ in China (2019)', China Highlights. Available at: www.chinahighlights.com/travelguide/article-qq.htm; see also: https://en.wikipedia.org/wiki/WeChat.

Weiner, J. (2019) 'How compassion builds better companies', Wharton University of Pennsylvania. Available at: https://knowledge.wharton.upenn.edu/article/linkedin-ceo-how-compassion-can-build-a-better-company/.

ACKNOWLEDGEMENTS

Thanks from Guy

The inspiration for this book has been my mother, Ruth. She was wise, insightful and gave me the gift of seeing the funny side of everything and intuitively understanding and helping others. She distilled in me love to other people and the importance of developing meaningful relationships.

She predicted that both Tami and I will jointly make a unique contribution to the field. This book is a testimony that she was right.

Co-authoring is a challenging project that would not have been completed without the help of many brilliant people. I am hugely grateful to many of my clients who can't be named for confidentiality reasons. Nevertheless, I would like to thank several people who have been instrumental in making this book into a reality. My profound thanks to my family who have been kind and sympathetic to this project, so my thanks to Iris, Ella and Ben, who are my sources of inspiration and energy. They did not just bring cups of tea and laughter when needed but are also a daily reminder of the power of love and connection. Many thanks to my dad, Eitan, and Dvori, who are ensuring that our family is always keeping in touch across Switzerland, US, Israel and UK.

My deep gratitude to Ashridge's assessment and psychometric and research teams, especially Victor Nilsson, John Pateman, Grace Brown, Emma Day-Duro and Carolyn Beard for outstanding and dedicated support. Erika Lucas for her brilliant and wise feedback on our drafts and overall wonderful encouragement throughout the writing process. John Higgins gave me inspiration and confidence that I can write this book as well as provided us with exceptional feedback. Mike Brent offered timely and generous help and vital input on key chapters. Erika Schofield shared important insights from her research that underpin Chapter 9 'Connecting across ages'. Special thanks for Dina Dommett and Katherine Murphey.

Thanks from Tami

The finest moment in the process of writing a book is the opportunity to explicitly thank my connections. The work itself felt like climbing a steep and slippery mountain. Then one day it was done, I stood at the peak and looked around. The view was breathtaking. It was all people. The path was full of endless eyes that saw me, arms that hugged, and voices that encouraged. I felt the power of *Connect* in every cell of my body. I was surrounded by a village, by my tribe, and I was never alone, not then, not now, not ever. That is what this book is about.

There is no way to acknowledge every person who contributed to this book without having a list longer than the phone book of New York City, so I will mention only those who had direct influence.

I must begin by expressing gratitude to my clients and to the clinicians I have been privileged to mentor. Your trust, courage and inner wisdom are the spine of *Connect*; your stories are hidden within every page. And I could not be a clinician if I did not stand on the shoulders of giants or grasp the hands generously offered by my supervisors, mentors and teachers. I thank my teachers at California Institute of Integral Studies, Dr Renee Emunah, Nina Strongylu and Audrey Martin, for giving me a solid clinical foundation. I thank my clinical and administrative supervisors who are making the world a better place, Kim Murphy, Katie Blank, Dr Jenny Love, Dr Lucy Fisher, Dr Suzanne Strisik and Dr Pat Sandberg. I add a special thank you to Anne Henry and Rebeca Farca, two brilliant clinicians who held me up during the roughest parts of the trail.

I will be forever grateful to those who gave me courage to write. Foremost, my friend and editor, Hava Rimon, emboldened me to be authentic and coached me in the art of writing. Sage Tremberth helped me to unravel the rules of the English language. Meg Thompson assisted me after I broke my arm.

Thank you to my teachers and colleagues at the Certificate in Psychedelic-Assisted Therapy Program at CIIS. Janis Phelps, Maria Mangini and Cathy Coleman, you are growing a movement that is transforming our field. Special thanks to my Narwhals friends.

True friendship is the ultimate manifestation of connection. None of this would be possible without having good, sincere and uncompromised friends. I am immensely grateful Charlene Lichtman for her wisdom and kindness, to Leslie Hercher for painting a new and exciting vision for the future. Gili Freiberg and Walter Naiman, you were there for years, through thick and thin. Your presence is a part of me even when we are separated by a big ocean.

I am blessed to have two families. My mother-in-law, Cora White, unwaveringly believed in me and everything I do.

My family of origin was my earliest connection. I thank my father, Eitan, who always supported me, even while baffled that his children chose to be psychologists. His wife, Dvori, has been committed to maintaining a large blended family that resides around the globe. Thank you for standing with us over the years.

I thank my brother and co-writer, Guy. When you were born, I was told by our parents that they got me a gift. You are a precious gift in even the toughest moments. Iris, Ben and Ella, I deeply love you, and I am grateful for you each day.

Ultimately, I thank the two women who are an integral part of my DNA. My late mother remains a source of endless inspiration. Mother, your wisdom, humour and sharpness are unmatched. Wherever you are right now, I hope you can see your dream come true.

To my wife, Flash – it is through living with you that I have experienced the healing power of love. You are the engine, the inspiration and the ultimate manifestation of *Connect*. THANK YOU.

And then there is Billy and Pita too. . .

From the both of us

We want to thank Dhanya Ramesh for being the mysterious person who supported us all the way from India. Your gentle inquiries and patience make a huge difference. Thanks to everyone in Pearson FT who worked on this book. With many of you we only connected through emails. We sincerely appreciate your contribution to the book and its concept.

A big thanks to Ewan Barr (Marine Mammal). Working with you was a true joy. Your creativity, sense of humour and ability to turn concepts into cartoons are a great contribution to the book.

Special thanks to Eloise Cook, our editor. It is probably the first time you functioned as both an editor and a family therapist. We are genuinely grateful for your kind guidance, your support and your patience.

Publisher's acknowledgements

7, 13, 31, 44, 73, 93, 117, 135, 164, 187 Ewann Barr: Ewann Barr **17 William James:** Quoted by William James **4 Totaljobs Group Ltd:** Mamo, E. (2018) – How to Combat the Rise of Workplace Loneliness, report. Retrieved from https://www.totaljobs.com/insidejob/how-to-combat-the-rise-of-workplace-loneliness/ **8 The Atlantic Monthly Group LLC:** Quoted by John Cacioppo, interview with The Atlantic Magazine in 2017 **10 Rudyard Kipling:** Quoted by Rudyard Kipling **11 BBC:** Robinson, N. (2012) Former RBS boss Fred Goodwin stripped of knighthood https://www.bbc.co.uk/news/uk-politics-16821650 **15 SmartBrief:** Yohn D. L. (2017),

Here's who is stalling your culture efforts, Smart Brief. Retrieved from https://www.smartbrief.com/original/2017/03/heres-who-stalling-your-culture-efforts **15 Harvard Business Publishing:** Zenger and Folkman (2014), Why Middle Managers Are So Unhappy, Harvard Business Review. Retrieved from https://hbr.org/2014/11/why-middle-managers-are-so-unhappy **17 BBC:** Bradford V (2013), Is modern life making us lonely? Retrieved from https://www.bbc.co.uk/news/magazine-22012957 **19 John Belgrove:** Quoted by John Belgrove **22 Ian Trenholm:** Quoted by Ian Trenholm **24 The Permanente journal:** Valerie Edwards, Charles L. Whitfield, Shanta R Dube, 'Childhood Abuse, Household Dysfunction, and Indicators of Impaired Adult Worker Performance', The Permanente Journal, January 2004 **28 Elias Porter:** Quoted by Dr Elias Porter **29 McGraw-Hill Education:** Hoffman, E,. Psychological Testing at Work: how to use, interpret, and get the most out of newest tests in personality, learning styles, aptitudes, interests, and more. US: McGraw-Hill, 2002 **42 Michael Jordan:** Quoted by Michael Jordan **45 J.K. Rowling:** Quoted by J.K. Rowling **69 Jawaharal Nehru:** Quoted by Jawaharal Nehru **70 Norman Augustine:** Quoted by Norman Augustine, former CEO of Lockheed Martin **83 Springer Nature:** Cooper, C. Flint-Taylor J. & Pearn M., (2013) Building resilience for success. A resource for managers and organisations. Palgrave Macmillan **85 Jim Whitehurst:** Quoted by Jim Whitehurst , CEO of open-source software maker Red Hat **87 Jill Flint Taylor:** This question is taken from Jill Flint Taylor **91 Mahatma Gandhi:** Quoted by Mahatma Gandhi **92 Anthony J. D'Angelo:** Quoted by Anthony J. D'Angelo **94 Sussex Publishers, LLC:** Becker-Phelps, D. L. (2019, July 8). Don't Believe Everything You Think. Retrieved from Psychology Today: https://www.psychologytoday.com/us/blog/making-change/201907/dont-believe-everything-you-think **97 Reinhold Niebuhr:** Niebuhr, R. (n.d.). The Serenity Prayer – What Does it Mean? Retrieved from Recovery on Purpose: https://www.celebraterecovery.com **99 Brené Brown:** Quoted by Brené Brown **103 Aristotle:** Quoted by Aristotle **103 Sun Tzu:** Sun Tzu (2016), Art of War, GENERAL PRESS **104 HarperCollins:** Marianne Williamson, (1992), 'A Return to Love' HarperCollins **105 Brené Brown:** Quoted by Brené Brown **106 Doug Larson:** Quoted by Doug Larson **106 Stephen R. Covey:** Quoted by Stephen R. Covey **108 HARPO PRODUCTIONS, INC:** The Oprah Winfrey Show Finale, (May 25, 2011), HARPO PRODUCTIONS, INC. **108 New Harbinger Publications:** McKay, David, and Fanning (2009) 'Messages: The Communication Skills Book' **114 Brené Brown:** Quoted by Brené Brown **118 Simon & Schuster:** Horsager, D. (2012). The trust edge: how top leaders gain faster results, deeper relationships, and a stronger bottom line. New York: Free Press. **122 Medium:** Parker, N. (2014, March 1). The Angel in the Marble. Retrieved from https://medium.com/@nilsaparker/the-angel-in-the-marble-f7aa43f333dc **123 John F. Kennedy:** Quoted by John F. Kennedy **124 Kim Scott:** TED Talk 'Radical Candor', Kim Scott **133 American Psychological Association:** Harry C. Triandis , (1989) 'The Self and Social Behavior in Differing Cultural Contexts', American Psychological Association, Inc. **137 McGraw-Hill Education:** Hofestede G, Hofestede, G.J., Minkov M. (2010) Cultures and organisations – software of the mind: Intercultural collaboration and its importance to survival. McGraw Hill companies **157 Brian Marshall:** List inspired by slide by Brian Marshall **162 The Atlantian:** Newspaper joke from the mid 1940s **165 Pew Research Center:** Pew Research Center tabulations of U.S. Census Bureau population projections released December 2014 and 2016 population estimates. **182 Deloitte Development LLC:** 'Rewriting the rules in the digital age' Deloitte, 2017 **186 Pearson Education:** Reitz, M. & Higgins J. (2019) Speak up. Pearson Education Limited **191 Pinder Sahota:** Quoted by Pinder Sahota **13 Iris Lubitsh:** Iris Lubitsh

INDEX